Time Shared

The Miracle of Transplant

Barba Covington McCarty

"Time Shared: The Miracle of Transplant." ISBN 1-58939-284-1.

Published 2002 by Virtualbookworm.com Publishing Inc., P.O. Box 9949, College Station, TX, 77842, US. ©2002 Barba Covington McCarty. All rights reserved. No part of this publication may be reproduced, stored in a retrieval system, or transmitted in any form or by any means, electronic, mechanical, recording or otherwise, without the prior written permission of Barba Covington McCarty.

Manufactured in the United States of America.

Dedicated to My Nephew

Lance Reed Cole
August 14, 1965 – June 6, 2002

Illness tells us what we are.
Anonymous (Italian Proverb)

Contents

Acknowledgements

Many persons have contributed to my successful liver transplant.

Grateful appreciation goes to:

Phyllis Brumley, who always listened, then laughed and cried in all the right places at all the right times. She made order out of chaos and ran my life while mine was on hold for so long.

April Hamilton Freeman, who spearheaded the fundraiser and blood drive and ran errands for me while I lived in Dallas and so much more laughing all the way.

My good friends who appeared and stayed with me when I needed them most during my illness at the hospital or while recovering: **Fay Stephens, Lucille (Mack) Larkin, Joann Smith Graber, Candy and Donnie Crutchfield, Judy Bryan, and Elizabeth Talley Howard.**

Sherri Covington, who is married to my cousin but is so much more; who drove me in the middle of a work week night in the rain and fog without sleep to Dallas when I got "the call" then stayed up until after surgery ended the next day.

My sisters, **Beverly:** who bought my food and supplies when I lived in Dallas and checked on me daily, and more, and let me stay at her home during recovery; **Betty:** who handled the worry department for everyone during the time after my surgery; she did it well and still does. She made special trips to take me to the food store and shopping when needed before and after my surgery and stayed with me at the hospital and during the later recovery with me and allowed me to stay at her home.

My husband, **James,** who did not have to do all he did for me during my illness.

Bobby Stevens, who talked me through a MRI with Phyllis, took me to doctor appointments, did the man-stuff around my house and came to my checkbook rescue when encephalopathy set its sights on my brain.

My friend **Mary Merritt** who spent the long, exhausting week of pre-transplant evaluation testing with me and made it *almost* fun.

My niece **Peggy** who stayed and cared for me after the surgery in 1995 when I was diagnosed with liver disease.

Wanda Konkle, aka Ben, my "other mother," and friend, who cooked so often so I would eat and listened to my fears and made me laugh when I thought I couldn't. I lost my good friend to a heart attack on July 5, 2003, the day I sent this book to my editor.

Those who contributed fiscally to the fund set up for me; some friends of my friends that I do not know and will never meet; and, to **Maxey Baptist Church** for paying the rent at my apartment in Dallas following my transplant.

My transplant surgeon, **Ernesto P. Molmenti MD,** no longer at Baylor University Medical Center. His knowledge and expertise have taken him to Johns Hopkins Medical Institution in Baltimore, MD where he Surgical Director of the kidney/pancreas transplant program.

The reason Baylor University Medical Center has such a fine transplant program, **Goran Klintmalm, PhD FACS,** Director of the Dallas Liver Transplant Program and the Director of Transplantation Services at Baylor University Medical Center at Dallas, Texas.

Dr. Klintmalm's associate and then Assistant Director of the transplant program at Baylor, **Marlon Levy, MD,** who without his and Dr. Klintmalm's medical knowledge and care since my transplant I could not have done, and cannot, do without. Dr, Levy is now director of a transplant program at Baylor All Saints Hospital in Ft. Worth, Texas.

My hepatologist, gastroenterologist, **Jeffrey Weinstein, MD:** on staff at BUMC whose medical knowledge and persistence kept me alive until an organ was available for my transplant.

The nurse coordinators: registered nurses who assisted in my evaluation, educating me and who kept up with where I was supposed to be when in the weeks following surgery and are still available today.

Ruth Ann Jones, my "liver buddy," for answering all the questions I had no matter when I had them. She is still here today answering my questions.

The nurses and staff on 14 Roberts Hospital, on the Baylor campus, so kind, so competent.

My Family Practitioner, **Paul Richard Bercher, MD,** who hung in there with me and treated me with compassion for twenty-five years of symptoms of unknown etiology until liver disease was discovered and is still here today for follow up care.

My donor's family, who made the choice to share life during the heartbreak of their loss.

My donor, who informed his wife of his wishes.

God...

To other recipients who allowed me tell their stories for informational purposes in this book.

And to the donor families who shared their stories for this book.

And to those who sent cards, made calls and said prayers for me and put my name on prayer lists all across the US, Canada and Mexico.

Introduction

*"Although I walk through the valley of Tzalmoves (Shadow of death);
I will not fear*
Tehillim (Psalms) 23:4

I first met Barba Covington McCarty online, when she asked me for a liver. A model liver. She contacted me because she thought that Novartis Pharmaceuticals (the company for which I work) might have such models available, because of our involvement in transplantation. Unfortunately, we do not, but I was so inspired by Barba's intention to educate people about organ donation through speaking that I helped her to obtain the models she wanted through a third party.

Little did I know at the time I was only seeing a tiny facet of the blazing jewel of inspiration that is Barba. I envisioned her as an enthusiastic organ recipient, touched by the gift that she had received, and eager to inspire others to think about donation so that someone else, like her, could benefit from the selfless gift of life.

She certainly is that; but not until I read the story that now lies before you could I appreciate how much more there was to Barba's history.

Here in an uncomplicated layperson's language, she tells of her own journey through the dreadful valley that King David describes in the psalm quoted above:

- Of years of weakness and discomfort that defied diagnosis
- Of everyday activities most of us take for granted, like going to the market, that left her so exhausted she could not even push her grocery cart through the checkout
- Of living a healthy and careful lifestyle and still ending up with a "bad" disease
- Of weeks on the waiting list, not knowing if perhaps, tomorrow, she would become one of seventeen people who die each day waiting for an organ to become available
- Of the unbelievable night when "the call" came and the story of the family that gave her the greatest gift at their time of their greatest sorrow
- Of surgery, and complications, and still more complications
- And, finally, of recovery and a second chance at life

Barba suffered the ultimate betrayal. Her body and even her brain, betrayed her because of viral hepatitis that destroyed her liver. Yet she emerged from the valley of that ordeal not embittered, but inspired and driven to inspire others so that more people might benefit from the greatest gift that a human being can give another, a gift for which the donor has no further use.

I invite you to walk with Barba through the valley, and to emerge with her into the sunlight of hope and promise and I would ask you, when your journey with her is over, to consider being an angel—an organ donor—and discussing it with your family and loved ones.

Please turn the page, and witness a miraculous journey.

Mark D. Grebenau, MD, PhD
August 29, 2002

Time Shared: *The Miracle of Transplant* *A Word Before You Read*

I f you believe in miracles, then you've most likely turned something over to God at some point, trusting that He would answer your prayers.

My story could be your story or the story of your loved one. Every sixteen minutes another person is added to transplant waiting lists in the United States.

My donor's story could be your story or the story of your loved one. Twenty-two thousand people will become brain dead in the United States of America this year.

My friend, Linda Miles' story, or my nephew, Dan's story, that I will tell you in this book, could be your story or the story of your loved one. Seventeen people die everyday while waiting for an organ.

And, my donor's story could be my story. I believe in miracles. I am alive today because of one, possibly several. I am also keenly aware that sometimes God says no. He has said no to my family as well; one story other than mine that involves liver disease I will tell you later in this book. Transplant recipients may be donors too, and for every one of us who have been blessed by being a recipient, the day will come when He will say no to all of us as well. I have instructed my family to see to it that I am a donor should God choose brain death as the way to say no to me. I have been blessed by transplant, and I would love to be another's blessing.

The odds that you or your loved one will need a transplant are much higher than your chance to become a donor. As of August 1, 2002 there are over 85,000, nearer to 86,000 people on transplant waiting lists in the USA and only 22,000 die of brain death per year. The odds are close to four-to-one that you or your loved one will need a transplant instead of that you or your loved may die a brain death and have the opportunity to be a life-saving donor. And, when the figures are tallied after transplants are received—when medical reasons rule out some donor organs and some of those who can, but do not, donate you are over **fourteen** times as likely to be in need of a life-saving transplant waiting on a list for an organ—that may not come—than you are to die of brain death and be able to donate.

How do you explain an illness to an illness-free person? You can't. It is not their fault, but their blessing, that they have not experienced chronic illness. Without the experience of severe chronic illness, there is no way someone can understand chronic illness.

I am writing this book to inform about chronic illness and to inform about organ and tissue donation so individuals may make informed decisions and to encourage people to have family discussions regarding donation. It is not my intention to convince anyone that donating is the right thing to do and that not choosing to donate is wrong. It is my intention to educate those who read about my transplant experience so they may make informed choices should the time of donation opportunity arise in their life. And, although I am not a doctor, it is my intention to inform future transplant patients what to expect as they make a long journey, as they struggle 24/7 to overcome what is literally an expiration date with an unknown date. The more awareness patients have about transplantation, the better they will do when they are hospitalized, recovering and maintain their life after transplant. You cannot be too informed.

Within the pages of information is my personal transplant story or maybe it is the other way around; within the pages of my story is information.

All recipients' stories are unique as are all donor stories. Writing about my transplant is risk-taking, which I am accustomed to. My story is about liver failure, chronic illness and near death. It is also about faith, hope, life and the power of caring for one another. As you page through this book you may chuckle quietly or laugh aloud, and you may cry. I will be telling you about an invisible illness that took a toll on me emotionally as well as physically (because of its invisibility the illness is discounted) and about the better times after it. I will take you from the time my illness began over thirty years ago— as far as it can be determined—and into my life today where I walk in a present that is my future; where God wrapped me in plastic bubble wrap and sent me to a place I thought I would never be.

1. Serendipity

I n Dallas, Texas ex co-workers, Ticha Hamilton and Jacky Mathews, along with a friend of Jacky, Tommy Welch and Ticha's husband, Derek, planned to attend a Sandi Patty concert together. Ticha, Jacky and Jacky's friend Tommy attended the concert. Ticha's husband, Derek, was absent. It was Friday, October 6, 2000.

Barba Covington McCarty

2. Finding Out

For this night an angel of the God I belong to and serve stood by me...
Acts 27:23

Our health to a large part depends on a well-functioning liver. If the liver fails, soon afterwards the kidneys fail, then the heart is damaged and serious neurological impairment occurs. This is all reversed by liver transplant.

Your liver, the largest organ in your body, is roughly the size of a football and weighs about three pounds. It lies in the upper right side of your abdomen, situated mostly under the lower ribs. The normal liver is soft, and it is connected to the small intestine by the bile ducts that carry bile formed in the liver to the intestines. The liver is a remarkable organ with multiple functions. Acting as the body's largest chemical factory, it has thousands of functions; filtering the blood is one of the liver's primary functions. Detoxification of drugs is the liver's second main role, synthesis and secretion of bile that coats the fatty foods we eat, making them easier to digest, is the third major role of the liver. Other jobs assigned the liver include; the production of enzymes, clotting factors, blood proteins, cholesterol metabolism, blood sugar concentration and hormone regulation. Because of its many functions liver disease can cause widespread disruption of body function. Liver dysfunction wrecks havoc throughout the body.

There are many diseases that may dictate a need for a transplant. I give you this rather long listing of diseases because there are those who think the only people requiring liver transplants are either alcohol or drug abusers. Among the diseases responsible for liver transplantation are the following: Hepatitis C Virus, Hepatitis B Virus, Urea Cycle Defects, Familial Hypercholesterolema, Alcohol Induced Cirrhosis, Glycogen Storage Disease, Autoimmune Disease, Primary Hyperoxaluria type 1, Cryptogenic Cirrhosis, Congenital Hepatic Fibrosis, Neiman-Pick Disease, Primary Biliary Cirrhosis, Familial Amyloidosis, Biliary Atresia, Hepatocellur Carcinoma, Primary Sclerosing Cholangitis, Hepatoblastoma, Alagille Syndrome, Hemangioendothelioma, Familial Cholestasis, Non-carcinoid Neuro-endoctrin, Drug Induced Liver Failure, Liver Tumors, Acute/fuliment Liver Failure, Budd-Chiari Syndrome, Alpha-1-Antrnrypsin Deficiency, Wilson Disease, Hemochromatosis, Tyrosinemia, Protoporphyria and Cystic Fibrosis.

Cirrhosis is a disease of the liver caused by gradual scarring over a long period of time. At first, liver cells become injured. If the cause of injury continues, the liver cells begin to die. Eventually, the normal liver cells are replaced by permanent scar tissue. This scar tissue cannot perform the many functions of the liver. If a liver continues to be injured by, as in my case, hepatitis C, HCV, the cirrhosis will get worse and more liver cells will stop doing their job. This can lead to death. A liver transplant is the ultimate treatment for cirrhosis.

In order to tell you my story, I need to back up a few years to when I was diagnosed with cirrhosis, and later, I will back up even further to when I contracted hepatitis twenty-four years before.

As far as it can be determined, my experience with liver disease began when I was twenty-two years old, but the first knowledge I had of it was on a hot July day when I was shivering cold in a patient room at St. Joseph's Hospital in my hometown of Paris, Texas.

I was already in a free fall after my husband James and I had split after twenty-nine years and nine months of marriage. When we split, I had no idea how to feel—but I had no doubt I had been confronted with death-in-life. My life was already on hold—I was alone with real life's harsh answer just around the corner.

* * *

I am a religious person, not fanatically religious, pretty liberal actually. However, I got right tired of angels during the decorating with angels craze that happened several years back. I remember as my friend Fay and I shopped, she bought several angels for others on her Christmas list then she asked me what I wanted for Christmas. I replied, "Just don't get me an angel. I'm tired of those damned angels everywhere."

Shortly afterwards, in November 1992, the first time I visited Dr. David Vanderpool's office, when I was referred to him by my family practitioner, Dr. Bercher, for a lumpectomy, I signed in on a clipboard that rested on a countertop next to a calendar with a religious picture and a Bible verse on it. I hadn't realized it until I sat down in the waiting room and picked up a magazine to read; but all the magazines had religious themes. There were religious themed-pictures on the north, south and east walls of the waiting room. As I went down the hall to the exam room, there was more religious artwork. The nurse seated me in the exam room where there were yet more religious-themed magazines and another picture, *Guardian Angel*—that painting of children walking across a bridge with an angel watching over them. I did not mind that my mind was flooded with Jesus and angels; after all, I wanted my doctor to have faith and belief in God. But, I also wanted my doctor to have faith in himself. About the time I let that not-quite-evil-but-somewhat-evil thought penetrate my brain, the nurse came and moved me to a room across the hall; on the wall in that room was *The Great Physician*—the picture of a doctor kneeling beside a patient's hospital bed in prayer. By then the thought about my new doctor having faith in himself and his work was firmly set in my head and was well on the way to becoming a full-blown evil thought.

I had not met Dr. Vanderpool before he entered the room. He stuck his hand out and introduced himself, "Mrs. McCarty, I'm Dr. Vanderpool; I believe Dr. Bercher referred you to us about a lump."

I looked at him as I shook his hand and said, "Just what religion are you?" He smiled. I could tell he was glad I had asked. "Church of Christ." His smile broadened, "Is that all right?"

I told him it was certainly all right, that I wanted my doctor to be a religious man, but I wanted him to have some faith in his work also. He smiled again and carried on as though he had all the faith in the world in God and himself. I have no doubt he did.

When I went back for my checkup after the surgery to remove a benign lump from my left breast, I took an angel I bought at the local art fair for his office. Surely there was room for one more.

* * *

When I went into the operating room holding area before my lumpectomy, an anesthesiologist told me that he had before him a test that showed liver dysfunction and asked me if I was aware of it. I wasn't. He said nothing else, and I was wheeled off to surgery. There were breathing complications afterwards in recovery, but I recovered and no big deal was made about the complications. I remembered it later and thought about asking Dr. Bercher about it the next time I saw him but never remembered when I was in his office.

In July 1995, I was referred to Dr. Vanderpool once again by Dr. Bercher for gallbladder surgery.

I had planned to have day surgery on Monday to remove my gallbladder while I still had health care insurance that would end when my husband, James, and I were divorced.

Call them coincidences call them happenings call them whatever you wish, the fact that I had gallbladder removal surgery before my husband and I had the final divorce hearing was the first of several miracles that happened concerning my liver.

Several relatives and friends, in fact every relative or friend who expressed an opinion, had suggested I wait until after the divorce hearing to have my gallbladder removed. After all, they said, I was distraught over the breakup of my marriage and would have Cobra insurance after the divorce for eighteen months. I refused all their suggestions.

The court date for the final hearing for the divorce was set for the following Monday after my gallbladder surgery.

I was rolled down the hall to the operating room elevator, followed by my friends, relatives and my estranged husband who leaned over as I was about to be rolled into the elevator and whispered in my ear, "I love you." Feeling loved but not believing it, I had no idea when I awoke that I would be thrust into a world different than any I had ever known or imagined—a world different not by divorce, that would last the rest of my life.

When I got to the operating room holding area yet another anesthesiologist said that my liver function tests showed dysfunction and asked had I been told of it. Suddenly, I remembered the anesthesiologist almost three years earlier asking me the same question, and I told him about it. Then I added no other doctor had ever mentioned it to me.

There was a long delay in the holding room afterwards as nurses and the anesthesiologist talked quietly among each other and finally changed me to a different operating room, put some hose on me that had not been prescribed and made arrangements for me to go to a different recovery room. I had previously been diagnosed with Lupus, so I thought they were taking precautions because of that, and I was glad.

* * *

There were breathing complications in the recovery room and some complications I was yet unaware of in surgery and my temperature had dropped drastically. When I awoke back in my patient room, I was inside a silver metallic bag where warm air was being electrically pumped in to the bag to warm me, but I was still shivering. My friend Mary was in the room along with several nurses and me.

Afterwards, I was hospitalized for eleven days because of the complications that occurred in surgery and recovery that I was still unaware of. Even more complications happened in the days that followed surgery that required I have a pump to remove yucky looking, yellow bile from my system.

I don't know exactly when I was told the news. When I felt better from the complications, Dr. Bercher entered my room. I did not think it strange that he came to my room even though he had referred me to Dr. Vanderpool for the surgery. On Dr. Bercher's heels were Dr. Vanderpool and two more white coats. White coats that I did not know. Four white coats at once mean something is wrong. Bad wrong. When I saw them enter my room, I knew I was about to be on the bad-news side of a doctor's visit. I was something I rarely am, speechless and uncharacteristically panicked, and none of the doctor's had said anything yet, not even hello.

Dr. Bercher began by saying there had been problems in surgery and that Dr. Vanderpool would explain them to me. He explained that he would not be caring for me for the new problems and that I would be in the hands of new doctors. Then, he left. I wanted to scream for him to stay, but, as I said, I was speechless even for screaming please stay at the man who had handled my health problems for almost twenty-five years.

Dr. Vanderpool introduced me to the other two doctors. One of them was Dr. Richard Dusold, a gastroenterologist, a doctor who treats liver diseases, in Paris, Texas, where I live. I was shaken, and to this day I have no idea who the other doctor was. I recall Dr. Dusold because I saw him later for further testing and consultations.

* * *

Dr. Richard Dusold is my kind of person and doctor. I have the persona of a person who has total control all the time. Dr. Dusold didn't pour on a sugar glaze. I don't either. He didn't beat around. I don't either. He laid it right out bare naked on the table; I've since done that a lot too. It took him less time to tell me what was wrong than it did for Dr. Vanderpool to tell me he was

Church of Christ. Dr. Dusold began with the bad part. I like that; tell me the problem then get to work *immediately* on the solution. But, nothing is immediate with liver disease.

As best as I remember, in the shock I was already in by the sight of four doctors entering my room at once, Dr. Dusold said something like, "You have a liver disease, a bad liver disease. You have had it at least twenty years, probably longer. Your liver is very damaged. You are looking at a liver transplant later; if you're lucky, you'll get one."

When he said the word transplant everything inside my brain shut down. I could hear his words but they were like words I was overhearing, like someone talking out in the hallway. The question—*What am I going to do?*— echoed in my mind. I thought I had my act together, but here I was in a straightjacket of fear and worry. He continued, "I understand you and your husband are separated. Do whatever it takes to stay with him and work it out. That insurance buys you a liver." Again he said, "*Whatever* it takes."

I was so shocked I couldn't even cry. I had no outward reaction when I heard the words "liver transplant." Dr. Dusold talked some more about the disease that I did not hear or comprehend. After a pause by the doctor, I said, "A transplant?"

He said once again, "Yes, so do *whatever* it takes to work this thing out with your husband." The words were reality bites.

My friend Mary, who was in the room when the doctors came, told me later that he asked me if I had questions. I didn't. She said that Dr. Vanderpool verified Dr. Dusold's news and also asked me if I had questions and told me if and when I did have questions to feel free to call him or Dr. Dusold. I had no idea what the questions were yet.

After the doctors left, I was silent for quite awhile. I could feel my heart beating where my neck joins my shoulders. I could hear it beating in my ears above the sound of abnormally staggered, labored breath air expelling from my nose. I was quivering inside. I recall asking Mary, "Did he say liver *transplant*?"

She said, "Yeah... he did, Barb."

I could not believe I had a liver disease. I wondered what I did to cause it; liver diseases were caused they didn't just happen. I waited quietly a while longer feeling my heart beat hard within my chest and listened to my loud heartbeat squishing in my ears with every breath I took, then I said to Mary, "Go get James." She left to go to James' apartment.

* * *

After she left, I felt as I had only one other time in my life. That other time was the evening after my mother's funeral. I overheard two of my older sisters, Mamie and Betty, and my brother, T.J., talking in the next room about what to do with Beverly and me—like it was going to be their decision—when my brother said, "I can take one of them, but I can't take both of them." I froze. I had lost my mother; I would die before I lost my little sister too. To this very day sometimes when I hear the song of my brother's voice on the telephone, I hear that tone he had when he uttered those words that scared me beyond anything before at the tender age of twelve. As I stood in the next room crying and shaking very shortly afterwards my father walked into the room where my sisters were packing clothing into laundry baskets and all hell broke loose. Bev and I didn't go anywhere.

* * *

I am grateful my room full of angels is crowded and there are some of the most unexpected angels in the room. My so-close-to-ex-husband-James showed up at the hospital a short time later just as my father did to keep Beverly and I together the day of my mother's funeral; he and I decided to stay married.

* * *

Dr. Vanderpool moved his angels to Nashville, Tennessee, not long after I was diagnosed with liver disease.

Later, my friend, Phyllis Stockton, gave me a lighted angel that serves as a nightlight. It sits on my TV today and is one of my favorite things.

I have had a lot of angels pass my way since the day years ago when Fay and I shopped and since my first visit in Dr. Vanderpool's Paris office. They weren't decorative angels in pictures on the wall but they passed my way.

* * *

I was confused, shocked, weak, helpless and very vulnerable. My life was totally out of control. I had no idea how much more out of control my life would get or how long before it would get better. I had taken a bad fall but I had to get up again less I miss out on life.

Later, when I did have questions of Dr. Vanderpool, I found out that during the surgery to remove my gallbladder, he had seen my damaged liver that sat next to my gallbladder. He had seen Dr. Dusold before he entered surgery and knew he was finishing a procedure in another operating room. He asked someone to get Dr. Dusold who was a gastroenterologist to take a look at my damaged liver. Dr Dusold scrubbed again and came in to look at my liver. They tried to get laproscopic pictures of my liver but were unable to when I became unstable on the operating table.

Dr. Dusold, a gastroenterologist, finishing up in the operating room close by was another angel sent my way.

The doctors determined I had cirrhosis, a term meaning a scarred liver. The parts of the liver that are scarred are non-functional, and mine was extensively scarred.

I was tested for several liver diseases, among them, hepatitis, which doctors were reasonably sure was the disease I had that caused the scarring, but all the test results were not in when I was released from the hospital.

Because of my experiences of so many years with so many symptoms, incorrect diagnoses and treatment I am an involved patient. I am a person who must be told everything about an illness. And, I must understand what I am told. I do not leave an illness to chance or in anyone else's hands, not even a doctor's hands. After years of dealing with a health care system that had failed me, without medical expertise I took it upon myself to learn all I could about liver disease, in particular the liver disease I had. When I was dismissed from the hospital, and while I waited for a battery of test results, I sought knowledge with a passion; fear of the unknown would not further my problem. I had lived over twenty years with symptoms of unknown etiology. I would not be in the dark again. I bought medical books, sent for literature, surfed the web and talked to others who had received liver transplants. My approach was to find out as much as I could about my disease and about transplant and to find out how to use the information I gleaned. I had to know the questions to ask when I saw Dr. Dusold in his office. In the years after I was diagnosed I learned all I could about my disease, but I did not obsess about it.

Barba Covington McCarty

3. But... I Did Everything Right

*God grant me the serenity
To accept the things I cannot change,
The courage to change the things I can,
And the wisdom to know the difference.*

He did. I had already accepted that I could not change the state of my health even before I knew what the diagnosis was for the unknown disease I had already had for so long. And, He had already given me a big mental file, that I titled "Things I Can Do Nothing About" to store most of it in. Over the next five years, as my illness worsened and as I waited for a transplant, that file grew and grew.

Actually, I felt relief that I had a diagnosis. It is much easier to know something is wrong even if it is bad wrong than to not know what the problem is. It was also good to know it was a physical problem too, and not something mental, which I will explain as you read farther into the book.

By quitting work I had already acknowledged my limitations and was beginning, reluctantly, to work within them; I had accepted the things I could not change. I no longer fought the many boundaries of my disease as I had for so many years before.

Possibly the best advice I have for those awaiting a transplant or those who suffer a chronic illness is to acknowledge your limitations and work with them. Acknowledge the boundaries of your disease and absorb them into your thoughts and mind so you can learn to work with them. Don't fight them. There is really no other choice, and fighting your limitations makes life much harder and uses your energy that is in short supply. "'Go with the flow" was the motto that Dan, my nephew who died of liver disease only fifteen months after my transplant, had followed for nearly forty years starting back in his hippie years. This was a philosophy he never dropped; he was practicing it way before we heard of Dr. Wayne Dyer, Dr. Phil or Oprah's "spirit" segments. Prayer and meditation enhance your ability to cope mentally. There is no cure; there is only healing when the body, mind and spirit work together to accept the disease. The coping skills of acknowledging your illness, meditating and prayer, are indispensable tools. Even when you accept that you are infected with hepatitis C virus (HCV) you will experience frustration, anger, depression and anxiety daily. It will take all the coping skills you can find, and still, there will be days when coping cannot be attained.

The effects of a compromised liver such as malaise, decreased appetite, extreme fatigue and depression take a toll on an individual's ability to perform activities of daily living. This reduced activity can lead to a decrease in flexibility, and endurance, and eventually a decrease in cardiopulmonary performance resulting in an increased surgical risk. A daily program consisting of regular exercise and normal activity for as long as you are physically able to do it can reduce complications and maximize your strength, flexibility, mobility, endurance and breathing. Backaches are common after liver transplant so exercises to strengthen your back are important. Back exercises were the only exercises I could do for a very long time before the transplant because I could do those in bed. I am glad I was able to continue the exercises as I did have back spasms post transplant. I feel the exercises helped.

Take a list of any questions you have to the doctor with you and leave a space below each question to write the answer the doctor gives you. If you don't understand a word, ask the doctor to spell it or get him to print, not write, (you know doctor's writing) the word for you to research later.

Understand your lab tests and know what they affect; it will be very important after transplant to understand your "numbers." All required lab tests are equally important, but knowing as much as you can about the tests, alkaline phosphatase (Alk Phos), AST (SGOT) and AST (SGPT) and GGT is very important. Know their ranges and what they mean. I made a card explaining what it means if any of my lab tests show to be elevated or down from their normal ranges.

* * *

When I went to Dr. Dusold's office for my first visit after I was dismissed from the hospital, I walked in and already waiting for me to arrive were two dear longtime friends, Phyllis and Mary. They had both taken off work, unbeknownst to me or to each other, to be at the doctor's appointment with me when I heard more of real-life's harsh answers.

On my first visit to Dr. Dusold's office, he told me that the tests had revealed that I had previously had hepatitis B virus (HBV) and hepatitis C virus (HCV). I had recovered from HBV but not from HCV, a common occurrence. Fifty percent of those afflicted do not recover from HCV. HCV had been damaging my liver for years, at least twenty he said.

In Dr. Dusold's office, I assured him that in all likelihood, during all of my forty-seven years, I had drank easily under one hundred alcoholic drinks; that's under two drinks a year, and that estimate allowed the benefit of the doubt to go to the alcohol. I told him even though I did grow up in the sixties I had never once tried intravenous drugs or any "recreational" drug that was not intravenous, including marijuana. I explained to him that I learned early on that the less medication one takes, the better and that I refrained from even taking over-the-counter medications unless absolutely necessary. I also explained that even though I was overweight, it was because of inactivity; I was careful not to eat foods that were bad for me. I had never used saccharin, because of its cancer warnings, or any artificial sweeteners; I didn't drink diet soft drinks for the same reason. I explained that I rarely drank soft drinks at all and that I drank mostly water. Because I was allergic to so many things, I used hair spray and deodorant that were not aerosol spray. I didn't eat much red meat. I ate low sodium, low protein, and a mostly vegetarian diet. I explained that if someone drank from my cup or used my lipstick, lip balm or toothpaste it was theirs; I would never use it again. I drank after no one. I didn't even drink from drinking fountains because I feel like they have other people's saliva germs on them. I did not have a tattoo and, although my thoughts concerning them could not affect my health, I explained that I did not understand those who did. I did not assault my body by spending my time in bars. I had not slept around. In short, I had not indulged in making destructive lifestyle choices. I had not lived a high-risk lifestyle.

Dr. Dusold listened as I told him all the things I did that were supposed to be good for me and to all the things I did not do that were supposed to be bad for me. When I finished expounding and singing my own praises of the right things I had done in my lifetime of forty-seven years, I asked him, "I did everything right...how can I have this?"

Then he said that I didn't have to drink alcohol or use drugs to get hepatitis. He said I did not have to do anything to get hepatitis. He said I could do everything right and still have it. I wanted an answer but an answer wasn't there because there was no answer. That day I put my disease itself in my "Things I Can Do Nothing About" file. The diagnosis satisfied me for a while. I was glad to finally have a diagnosis for the many symptoms of unknown etiology that had plagued me for so long. But, still, even now, occasionally, I pull out that file and try to figure out how I got this disease.

From my research on the Internet, booklets I had ordered and in medical books, I entered Dr. Dusold's office with a lengthy list of questions and my mind mostly made up not to take Interferon, a chemotherapy for treating HCV, and I told him so even before he brought it up. He said he must explain all the available options of treatment for my disease. He did a rather lengthy explanation while I took notes. When he was finished I asked him, "If I was your forty-seven-year-old wife with cirrhosis as advanced as mine would you want her to take Interferon?"

His reply was, "You may try Interferon if that's your decision. There is about a 5 percent chance that it might help in your case. And, you would be very sick while you take the treatment. The damage is already done to your liver." The reason for his not recommending Interferon is that my liver was already severely damaged and the treatment would have made me sicker and not helped, nor cured, my disease. Had my liver disease just begun, Dr. Dusold might have recommended treatment with Interferon, since it might have stopped the progression of the disease. I was glad he thought as I did about Interferon, but I had no idea the only alternative was transplant, even though it had been mentioned when I was hospitalized.

When I left his office, I was still bewildered as to how I contracted hepatitis B and C. I had not contracted hepatitis from making the wrong choices, so why did I get it? Previously, I had worked doing the clerk's work for court-ordered drug and alcohol commitments. From that job, I was acquainted with drug addicts and alcoholics. Why did I, who had never once used or abused drugs, get this disease? Why did I, who had used alcohol so sparingly, to the tune of two drinks a year... maybe, get this disease? When I left Dr. Dusold's office, I still did not know, and to this day, I do not know and never will. That fell into my file of "Things I Can Do Nothing About." Some people do not learn that until late in life; I had learned it early in life at the age of twelve when my mother died.

Shortly afterward, Dr. Dusold moved away from Paris, Texas. I was devastated. His knowledge and expertise have taken him to Scott and White Clinic in College Station, Texas.

Even before I was diagnosed, the disease already ran my life and affected every aspect of my daily living; I no longer lived as I had in the past; I no longer lived for a future. I lived in the present; the right-that-minute present, handling the day-to-day care of cirrhosis caused by HCV even though I had no idea it was the cause of my illnesses. I had gotten so ill that I no longer had a passion for living. I no longer wrote, and I no longer traveled.

My life was a blank check and had been for a while. At this point, dying was not an option for me although my expiration date was close. So, I set out to stay alive.

4. Friends, Wonderful Friends

Think where man's glory most begins and ends,
And say my glory was I had such friends.
William Butler Yeats

F riends make the long hard journey of transplant easier. I am so lucky to have many.

Friends are different than family. They have no obligation whatsoever, whether real or imagined, to stand by you or support you. They are there of their own giving selves. And, it takes all of them to make it through transplant.

Every friend is different; they all have different talents, time commitments, and amounts of money they can expend on running about for someone else, or possibly, different ideas of what they can and will do. When I think of my friends, I think of Hillary Clinton's book titled *It Takes a Village.* There is no correct or incorrect way to be a friend; every friendship is different, and every friend is needed. Some can and will stay with an ill person, some are cooks, some are go-getters, some are organizers, some are drivers and some are workers. They are all needed.

Some friends make it through the big story, the transplant surgery, then wane. Some are there for talk support. Some are workers and some are givers of money, goods and even their own blood. Some make it all the way. Some stay because they have knowledge from experience of what it's like to have someone in long-term care and some have a compassionate heart and some have both. Donnie and Candy had both; after losing a son to cancer just a short time before, they came and stayed at Twice Blessed House with me more than once.

Two of my friends, Judy and Liz, worked weekdays and came to stay with me on weekends, both more than once. Liz brought cooked meals to me before I was hospitalized. Judy came on her lunch hour and cut my hair before it quit growing.

Fay came and stayed days at a time with me multiple times and many times cooked food and delivered it to me when I was ill. Once when she was staying with me at Twice Blessed House, she became afflicted with vertigo. I could not get her to leave, possibly because she couldn't stand up and she might have been arrested, being mistaken as drunken.

My "other mother" and friend, Ben, cooked many meals and had me over to eat when I would have otherwise not eaten. She came and stayed nights with me when I was at my sickest and assured me that she had prayed, and I was, indeed going to get a liver in time. Then she would turn it all around and make me laugh at my worry.

Bobby who saved my checkbook also repaired my garage door, checked on my car problems, took me to doctor's appointments, talked me through the MRI with Phyllis and went to the food store and Wal-Mart for me several times after he got off work at eleven at night.

My cousin Ira mowed my yard, as did Phyllis's son, Brian and his wife, Joi.

My lifelong friend, Joann, who works as a paid caregiver, came on her week off to stay with me at the hospital simply as a friend asking for no pay, twice. She also made special trips to Paris, to stay with me days at a time when I was so ill before the surgery and shaped my positive attitude toward my illness, which I will talk about later in this writing.

Another of my "other mothers," Mack, who is Phyllis's 86-year-old mom, came and cared for me at Twice Blessed House as though I was her own child.

Monica, Phyllis daughter, took a day off work to bring me home from the hospital after a short stay.

My friend, Phyllis Stockton, came and stayed the night with me at a call's notice more than once when I was severely ill before transplant.

Maxey Baptist Church paid the rent at the apartment in Dallas for the three months I had to live there post transplant.

April came to Paris often from the Dallas area to be with me. She took me to appointments, brought food that I might eat. While I was hospitalized and living in Dallas afterwards she picked up items I needed. She spearheaded the blood drive and the fundraiser that she and Phyllis handled together. Anyone who knows her, or works with her, even some of her customers have been asked for blood for me. April makes her living as salesperson and she is already selling copies of this book before it is sent to a publisher. And, she did it all with humor, laughing and actually making severe illness almost fun for me.

Expenses during the illness before and after the transplant are massive even with insurance paying the hospital bill. People who were friends of my friends, that I have never met, sent money to me from April's effort and initiative to have and manage the fundraiser. Every penny was appreciated and used to handle the many added expenses for trips to doctors in Dallas, the many different medications that were tried and the living expenses while I was in Dallas three-and-a-half months after the surgery.

One couple that I do know, and are long-time friends, Pat and Burnas, sent money to me that they "made" while gambling in Tunica, Mississippi. I have a beautiful letter from Pat, to April, explaining about how they got the money.

In the letter Pat said they wanted to contribute a thousand dollars to me but their bank account was not in a position to just write a check. So, they contributed some "seed money," $180.00, to gamble with, and pledged the first one thousand dollars gained to the "Barba fund". At the end of day one,

Burnas had $949.00 in the pledged fund, including the seed money. He had gained $769.00 of the desired one thousand dollars. The next morning he went back down to the casino with faith that he would make the rest of the goal of a thousand dollars. He made it, plus enough to pay for their gas and trip including the seed money. They sent a check for one thousand dollars to April for my fund.

In the letter I am reading that Pat wrote to April, explaining where the money came from, she says, "God sent it… literally." I am inclined to believe that God works in mysterious ways through wonderful and caring people.

You will find that the truly busy person is the person who makes time for others in life; the people who volunteer, the committee members who take on more jobs, the person who works two jobs, the person who teaches a class in addition to all they already do, the person who has a finger in many pies is also the person who voluntarily shows up for a sick friend.

There was no rest for Phyllis Brumley, who had been there all along. She took several days off from work to take me to Dallas to doctor's appointments, and ran my life while I was away, coordinated the stays of others while I was hospitalized and lived in Dallas three-and-a-half months. She is one of those folks who has a hand in many committees and joins in any effort to help her community; she is on the fair board, more than one cemetery committee, her community center committee and puts an extra effort in the kids at the high school where she works and in FFA projects; she does the reunions for her high school class and is a married woman running her own home and life. I have never once heard Phyllis say to anyone, "I can't; I'm busy."

These are all friends who gave freely of themselves; none were paid fees to do a job. I am aware how blessed I am to have them and to have had so many who made it all the way with me.

And, yes, there are the friends you are positive will be there but will not be; they will be the ones who talk about how busy they are. Those who really are that busy don't have the time to talk about their busyness—they are too busy.

A word to those who are ill and awaiting the transplant when someone will have to be there with you very often and very long—take the people who volunteer to help up on their offers. You may feel like you must save them for later when you are hospitalized and recovering after transplant, but don't, I did not always accept help but have since learned that it is a must. I allowed those who volunteered to do only the things that had to be done; the small jobs I would not let them do. When someone volunteers to assist you they may not know what you need done. When someone asks, "What can I do for you?" or "Is there anything I can do?" or "If you need anything let me know" they do mean it. It is hard to delegate what has been your responsibility for a lifetime, especially the small jobs. But, if you don't get the small jobs done, they become large jobs over time.

Since I am now proficient at being ill, I'm giving lessons on taking friends up on their offers of help to my friend Carol who is going through chemotherapy now for carcinoma of the lung. For those waiting for a transplant, the time when help will be needed more is coming; the crisis time comes in the months before and after the transplant, but for my friend with lung cancer, the crisis time is now. She keeps saying, "I know I'm going to get sicker and need them more then." She is probably right; and we, her friends, will be there. True friends are there, and friends she doesn't even know she has yet will be there too. Another friend of Carol's has a different take on it. She says the person helping will get a blessing and would you cheat someone out of a blessing?

Those friends who provide laughter before and during chronic illness or serious surgery are the same friends who provide the laughter during and after transplant.

I am not a cat hater; I am just not a cat lover. Well, maybe I am a cat hater; I couldn't stand them even if I wasn't allergic to the fluffy little balls of fur and aggravation, sliding around your legs or quietly leaping upon the furniture beside you but I have many friends who have them.

Then there's Felix.

In February 1982, I was lying in my hospital bed after having a hysterectomy, and I heard a rustling of paper and looked around to see an arm sticking around the corner holding a picture of the cartoon character Felix the Cat pointing his sharp claw to the right. At the bottom of Felix's picture was the caption, "Would you be very upset if I asked you to take your silly-assed problem on the down the hall?" The arm and hand attached to Felix was my friend and cat lover, Mary. I laughed until I had spasms at the incision site and had to have medication to calm them and me. When I was dismissed, I took Felix home with me, knowing that someday I would get to use him when Mary was hospitalized. I have. A year after I experienced spasms from laughter at Felix and Mary, I finally got the chance to take him back to Mary; I taped him to the door of her hospital room and didn't tell her he was there. She kept hearing laughter and giggling outside the door, and finally, a nurse told her Felix was on the door. Mary brought him back to me another year later in February 1984 when I was admitted for tests before HMOs stopped us from being admitted for tests. I sent Felix back her way once again when she got a concussion from the trunk lid of her car hitting her head when she and her husband Billy had car trouble on the road. For this visit, I added to the caption to make it read, "Would it be asking too much to ask you to take your silly-assed problems on down the hall? I have a headache?" I sent Felix over again to visit Mary when she had back trouble in February 1991. In September 1993, Mary skipped the fun with Felix, and he missed my hospitalization after I was in a car accident and sustained a broken neck. When I asked about him Mary said the injury was far too serious for Felix. It was. But, when Mary got rear-ended in 1994, I took Felix to check on her own neck injury, a whiplash. In July 1995, after I had gallbladder surgery and the liver disease was discovered, Mary thought again that it was too serious for Felix so she mailed him to me at home once I was better, with a note written above his head saying that Mary thought I needed a cat and that she was looking for one for me. While I was hospitalized and finally doing well after my transplant surgery, she brought a copy of Felix to my room and tacked him up on the bulletin board. The Felix paper poster is getting tattered and yellow, but Felix is still the only cat that makes me laugh.

* * *

But friendship is precious not only in the shade, but in the sunshine of life;
and thanks to a benevolent arrangement of things
the greater part of life is sunshine.
Thomas Jefferson

Barba Covington McCarty

5. End-Stage Liver Disease (ESLD)

But the angel said to them, "Do not be afraid...
Luke 2:10

*e*nd-stage liver disease means the worst has been postponed. It means you are literally caught between life and death, and you are much closer to death. It means you have fallen hard and there is no energy to get up, not even for life, so you must let the thoughts that form your attitude be the ruler of the rest of your life or until you get a transplant, whichever comes first. You cannot take your eyes off the goal of transplant. There is no past and there is no future. You live only in the moment. The disease that ran my life so long now denied my life to me and made me a prisoner in my own house, just my sidekick, cirrhosis and me.

For years, I have had a telephone in every room in the house, including the bathrooms. I was terrified of becoming incapacitated from fainting, a fall, a throat closure or a bleed and being unable to get to a telephone to call for help.

I have in my garage a shelf that will hold sixteen twenty-four packs of toilet tissue. That rack is always full and the first comment from anyone who enters my garage is about "all that toilet tissue." I have that rack there, and it is full because for years I bought tissue only when I was able to get out and buy it; often I could not get to the store for necessary items because I was too weak or sick, therefore, every time I was where there was tissue for sale I bought it. Buying tissue at every shopping trip is a habit I still have today. Since my transplant I have made many adjustments in my mind, and there are still many that have not been made; the tissue thing is one of them. Another is not waiting until I am very sick before I go to the doctor, now it can be the difference in life and death. I can no longer do what I did before and not go as soon as there is problem. In ESLD I have been too ill to even go to the doctor many times.

Another adjustment not made is when I go out to eat and am asked if I like certain foods my answer will often be no, then I think about the fact that I have not tried that food since my transplant, so I really do not know because I for so many years I did not like any foods.

In September of 1993, almost two years before my hospitalization that resulted in finding out I had a cirrhotic liver, my condition had deteriorated to the point where I quit my job I loved as a civil/probate clerk in the county clerk's office. Although at forty-five years old my body had served me notice by excessive tiredness, I was not eager to begin a gone-shoppin' retirement; in fact when I quit work I could no longer shop. In fact, I already knew I was too ill to go shopping, even if I wanted to or needed to. I just would not lay down living. My husband and I were still together, and I had been advised by Dr. Bercher to quit working a few times before. He would say things like, "You don't have to work, do you?" or "Have you thought about quitting work?" I had been diagnosed with lupus and had gotten to the point that I was afraid if I didn't work I might become incapacitated and could not function day to day. My ego demanded that I be "normal." I was not willing to exchange life for memories. Because I was afraid of incapacitation, I dragged around, preparing supper, doing housework, and, known only to me, crying a lot. I felt so bad doing the things I had to do to show that I was not incapacitated or sick even to my husband. My defect could not be glimpsed by anyone. To avoid talking about my illness when someone asked, "How are you?" I replied, "I'm just great."

I went from a high-energy woman who drove a motorcycle and moved the refrigerator, by myself, to clean underneath it to one who could barely make it through the grocery store while holding onto the grocery cart for stability to buy groceries. It was a slow process, but my life had changed. Cirrhosis caused by HCV is a slow process, thus it encourages postponement of the seriousness of the disease even by those who live in the world now where diagnosis is made so much sooner.

Over time I had to quit being the ordinarily independent woman I had always been. I could no longer keep up with the rest of my world. I had to quit the daylong shopping trips to Dallas with Mary that I had enjoyed for so many years. Movie marathons (3 or 4 in one day) with my nieces were a pastime until I no longer felt like driving to Dallas, seeing the movies then driving home again. My health dictated that I quit doing so many of the things that defined me; like driving four hundred miles alone to visit my sister in Amarillo then she and I getting in the car and driving four hundred more miles with me doing all the driving. I could no longer rent a car with my cousin and drive, unafraid, in Los Angeles with no guide. I could no longer walk and carry my carry-on luggage through D-FW airport. I could no longer park and walk to the terminal without a bag at all. My disease changed my personality and my whole way of life. Before I quit work, many were the days I came home from work, went straight to bed and stayed there until time for work the next morning. During that time, I often cried soundlessly. Still, I would not give up and quit work. I am of the belief that if you fall, and stay down, life will pass you by. Quitting work to me was the staying down after a fall I was trying so hard to prevent.

I quit work at the county clerk's office on September 23, 1993. The first stumble after I quit work happened a week later, on September 29th when my husband, James, and I had a car accident less than two miles from our home. We hit one of three horses that were being chased by a woman and her children down the highway, at night, toward traffic. The people were trying to get the horses back in the stable that they had escaped from when one of the horses being chased toward traffic ran out into the highway. My neck was broken.

A lifelong friend, Rodger Edelhauser, an off duty EMT, was home when he heard on his scanner the information concerning a 911 call about a couple in a blue Toyota injured when they had hit a horse on Highway 195. Rodger had been monitoring the scanner for a while and knew all the ambulances were tied up on other calls. His wife told me when they visited me at the hospital, "Rodger was putting his coat on, walking out the door and talking all at the same time." She said that he said, "'That sounds like Barba and James' and he was gone." He came on his off duty time to the scene of our accident and rode in the ambulance with me to the hospital, I am told, talking and comforting me all the way. Was Rodger, an angel performing a miracle off duty? If you ask me, I'll tell you he is.

And, Dr. Ed Schaeffer was behind us in a car and made sure I wasn't moved, possibly another angel passing my way.

I spent eighteen months recovering, with no effects whatsoever, from that broken neck. Yet another miracle.

* * *

Almost two years later, in July 1995, I had been out of the hospital only a couple of days, after being diagnosed with liver disease. My niece Peggy was staying with me during the recovery period when I had an attack where my airway closed and I could not breathe. I had already experienced my first jaundice while hospitalized after the gallbladder surgery. My belly, thighs, tummy and abdomen were a dark golden yellow. Lots of fluid had built up on my belly; it was the first time I had been prescribed fluid removal medications—for what was described to be bile buildup caused by leakage of the liver in the area where my gallbladder had once lay against my liver.

When I had the throat closure I was alone; Peggy had gone to the food store. I ran to the kitchen and poured a glass of ice water over a dishcloth and put it on my throat. I got better and the attack was over when Peggy came in. We went to the hospital, and I was given an injection of Benadryl. On the way home from the hospital, Peggy insisted I needed to eat and get out of the house, so we stopped to eat at a Mexican restaurant. As came around to open the passenger door, I reached up near my waist in back and felt something was wet and told her. Teasingly, she said in a harsh tone, "You're not wet get out we are eating here." When inside we ordered, and as we waited for our food to arrive, I felt behind me at my waist again and was dripping wet; I was glad I was wearing a black dress that wet could not be seen so clearly on. We drove home from the restaurant and by the time we got there, the car seat was soaked wet underneath me. When we got inside and checked, there was yellow fluid speedily dripping from a pore on my upper right buttock. It dripped for hours. At first, James, Peggy and I thought the fluid was leaking from the site of the Benadryl injection, but it had not been given in my right hip. It was an unbelievable scenario, and there was no medical explanation for it but being the patient that I am, who simply must know everything and why, I was all but demanding an answer from Dr. Bercher. He said if there were fifty doctors here they could not tell me why it happened; there was no medical explanation. Perhaps it was another angel relieving me of jaundice and fluid.

A day or so later, I had another throat-closure attack. After struggling to do the Heimlich method for choking on myself, by using the back of a recliner then a kitchen chair with no success, Peggy heard me and tried the Heimlich method also with no success. I ran toward the car, and my niece started driving towards the hospital. As I struggled to suck for air I turned the air-conditioning vent to blow air directly into my face. As we drove my throat opened, and I could breathe again. Although this event was worse than the one a few days before and I was very weak after it when the attack was over, I saw no need to go on to the hospital. But, we did. It was mentioned that I could possibly be having an anxiety attack with all that was happening in my life at that time—marital separation, gallbladder surgery and severe liver disease had been diagnosed and a possible upcoming transplant had been mentioned. I was definitely anxious after the throat closures.

* * *

In late 1998, fluid problems were increasing for me. Dr. Weinstein prescribed new fluid removal medication, Aldactone, for fluid that was building up on my right lung. On the way, while driving to meet a friend and attend a New Year's Eve southern-gospel-singing event, I had to roll the car window down to breathe even though it was extremely cold outside. I thought it might be the perfume that I had lightly sprayed right before getting in the car. I got out of the car in the freezing cold and went inside where I met my friend and were seated in the packed church. As the second song was being sung, I had another sudden throat-closure attack. I had no idea how I was going to get out of the packed church sanctuary with chairs in the aisle and people standing in the foyer entrance. I bounded for the back when all of a sudden a very tall young man with dark hair grabbed me from behind and began the Heimlich procedure. It wasn't working, and I finally struggled free of him, and we both ran outside the door in the freezing cold where there was an ambulance parked with two emergency medical technicians getting out of it. Instantly, my breath was somewhat better, but the EMTs and the tall man insisted I go to the hospital. I told them I had experienced this problem before, and now it was over, so what good would it do for me to go to the emergency room after it was over? They wouldn't take no for an answer. I promised them I would go directly to the hospital since I could drive. The tall man who tried the Heimlich procedure was an off-duty EMT. Three more angels.

A friend who had seen all the commotion had come over to see what was wrong with me and volunteered to get my car from the parking lot. She drove it directly onto the church's snowy, soggy volleyball court and sunk my car axle deep. The three EMTs and three other men picked my car up and moved it off the volleyball court. I was weak and shaky, so I went directly home, not to the hospital as I had promised the EMTs.

I dreaded calling and interrupting Dr. Bercher's New Year's Eve, but I was too scared not to call him. He was his always-wonderful self and prescribed that I discontinue taking Aldactone and prescribed a smaller dosage of Amiloride and Prednisone in its place to take along with the Lasix I was taking already. After this third attack of throat closure, I figured out that cold somehow helped the problem. During the first episode, I had applied ice-cold water to my throat, then the second time, I had turned cold air from the car's air-conditioning vent to blow in my face and on the third attack, I had run outside the church into the very cold air of New Year's Eve 1998. I tucked that thought into the emergency file in my brain.

* * *

I had no more attacks until 2000 when I experienced more ascites to my swollen belly and fluid medications were changed and increased once again. I was home alone late at night, actually early in the morning after a night of no sleep, when I had another throat closure on January 26, 2000. I tried the Heimlich procedure on the back of a kitchen chair until I thought I had broken my ribs; if given the choice of air to breathe or broken ribs you will choose breath. I suddenly remembered the cold thing, threw a glass of water on my face and ran outside. When the water and air hit, I was better and decided I would live even though I kept gasping for breath while standing outside in the cold January night air. This time I only rested afterwards, no sense in waking Dr. Bercher or going to the hospital again.

* * *

Sixteen days later another throat closure happened on February 11, 2000. Instead of trying to do the Heimlich procedure on my still bruised ribs I ran outside in the cold night air and gasped for breath longer than ever before. I fanned the air with my hand and started to run, as best as I could then, across the street to a house where a light was on. I became exhausted and fell in my driveway. As I lay there thinking I had taken my last gasp of life, my breath returned once again. I was so weak that I had to lie in the driveway, freezing cold for awhile before I could get up to go back inside. This time I waited to call Dr. Bercher's office the next morning and was seen right then. An emergency injection of Epinephrine was prescribed for me in case I experienced another attack.

Six days earlier I had finished taking the Prednisone prescribed by Dr. Bercher after the throat closure I had on January 26th. I started back taking Lasix and Amiloride for fluid build up after the Prednisone was finished. Amiloride was discontinued after the event of February 11th. It was decided that since I had just finished Prednisone for the January 26 attack that it had not worked its way out of my body and therefore had protected me against attacks even though I was taking the offending medication, Amiloride.

Throat closures are scary. During my disease, I was most scared when I had those attacks.

After the event of February 11, 2000, I became hoarse and experienced severe laryngitis. I was referred to a throat specialist for a check up of my vocal cords which proved to be all right, then I was referred to a gastroenterologist who refused the request for an endoscopy because the varices were too fragile the last time he had done an endoscopy, so he saw no reason to chance complications by injuring the area and possibly causing a bleed. The severe laryngitis and hoarseness continued until early April 2000.

6. In the Beginning

J ames and I decided to start our family while he was in the U.S. Army. I never became pregnant, and we continued our efforts to become parents when we got back home to Paris, Texas in February 1969 after James' discharge from the army.

Still unable to get pregnant, in September 1969, I decided to go to an obstetrician for advice. I called both of the OB/GYN doctors in town at that time and was told by a receptionist at both offices they were only taking new patients who were pregnant. Both doctors were trying to leave the gynecology branch of their practice in favor of concentrating on the obstetrics branch. After explaining to Dr. Bagwell's office assistant that I was trying to get pregnant, she told me there was a new doctor coming to Paris and that his office was opening the following week. She gave me his name and telephone number.

I called the office of Paul Richard Bercher, MD, Paris' first family practitioner. I was Dr. Bercher's patient on the second day his office opened. He was young, mild mannered, articulate and very compassionate. I felt at ease with him immediately.

In the next thirty years that followed, I would visit Dr. Bercher's office hundreds more times, as he treated me for many symptoms of unknown etiology. He referred me to specialists some who would dare not say "I don't know" and give up and to those who did say "I don't know" after testing for anything that might remotely be connected to their specialty.

My husband had, and still has, a great interest in anything with wheels and engines; motorcycles, tractors and cars in general but particularly street rods, modified antique cars. Less than four years after my first visit to Dr. Bercher, in 1973, he purchased a white Corvette that my husband was positive we bought for him with money from my medical bills. On a visit to Dr. Bercher's office where James accompanied me and went back to the car for something we left in the car when Dr. Bercher arrived and parked his new 'vette. Of course, James approached him and took a close look at the white Corvette. Later that evening when we arrived at Billy and Mary's, with great excitement James told Billy, "You won't believe what I bought today." Of course Billy had no idea and James told him, "A brand spanking new white Corvette" and he proceeded to explain in detail, as only one street rodder to another can do. When he finished Billy said, "Well, where is it? Why aren't you driving it?" James said, "I'm letting Dr. Bercher drive it." Dr. Bercher still has that white Corvette and a picture of it in his office today, and my husband still thinks we bought it.

Many times over the years the thought of changing doctors entered my mind but only briefly each time as I liked that Dr. Bercher kept up with the latest medical technology. In my heart I knew he was doing all that could be done for me, after all, the specialists were not coming up with solutions to my many symptoms either. He was always there if I called him after hours, which didn't happen unless I waited too long—a problem for me even today. He was familiar with my many allergies and knew my body and its reactions almost as well as I did. Having chronic illness had made me very aware of my body. I thank God for Dr. Bercher. It's hard to tell; he may have been sent to Paris just to care for me or so my husband could buy him a white Corvette.

James resumed attending college during the day to become an engineer and worked at Campbell's Soup Company on the graveyard shift. I was attending Paris Junior College and working part time as a cashier at the Dairy Kream, a small, locally owned eatery. I was twenty-two.

It's hard to tell when it, hepatitis C, all started but if you ask me I will tell you it started on a cold January day in 1971. Roy, the owner of the Dairy Kream, went home after the noon rush for a rest, as he did every day. After his rest period, he came back for the busy night. I felt fine when Roy left for his afternoon rest, but while he was gone, I suddenly got a high fever and was shaking with chills. I tried to wait out Roy's two-hour rest period before going home, but I couldn't. I called him at home, and told him about the fever and how sick I was and asked him to come back so I could leave. Roy didn't get in a hurry; after all I had been fine when he left less than an hour before. When he got back to the Dairy Kream I was shivering cold even though I was wrapped in my heavy coat and standing in front of the large heater turned on high.

Later that night, because my temperature was so high, Dr. Bercher admitted me for my first ever hospitalization that lasted fourteen days. Phyllis, who ran my life while mine was on hold at transplant time, was there then too. The diagnosis was "a mononucleosis-type thing." As far as it can be determined that mononucleosis-type thing was the beginning of my liver disease.

Back when I contracted the disease in 1971, there was no test or diagnosis for hepatitis C. The disease was not identified until 1989. There was not a test to screen donated blood that may have been tainted with HCV until 1992. If you had a blood transfusion before July 1992, you may have HCV. As many as three hundred thousand Americans may have been infected this way before the test for hepatitis C was developed enabling blood used for transfusions to be screened for HCV. This is no longer the case. Now transfusion-associated cases of HCV occur in less than one per million transfused unit of blood.

Your liver doesn't let you know it is sick until it, and you, are almost at the end of the rope. Listen to your body—it may be telling you something by its first subtle signs of unexplained illnesses.

Before the hospitalization, I was rarely sick even with a cold. I had only seen Dr. Bercher to see why I was unable to get pregnant. After the mononucleosis-type thing, I was sick often with flu-like symptoms of fever and joint pain, but I didn't have the coughing and nasal symptoms. The fever would last three or four days and taper off. The joint pain always lasted longer. It was a come-and-go flu-like illness that occurred repeatedly.

Over the next twenty-four years, I was tested many times by many different doctors, diagnosed and misdiagnosed, by those same doctors, with many illnesses: arthritis, rheumatoid arthritis, myalgia, fibromyalgia, pituitary tumor, Epstein-Barr, chronic fatigue syndrome and lupus. I had frequent kidney infections and many allergies to medications. Even now, misdiagnosis is common for hepatic patients. The same endocrinologist in Dallas who diagnosed me with lupus said that I had a "yuppie illness" and I needed a mental evaluation. In other words, with all his knowledge and ego, if he couldn't find out what was wrong with me then it must not be there, and therefore, I must be nuts. On my way for checkups at Baylor, when I drive past the street to his office I still have a terrific urge to go by his office and pull up my shirt and show him my scar as proof that there was something wrong; and it wasn't a yuppie illness in my mind. But if I did he might surely think a mental evaluation was in order. Thank goodness Dr. Bercher did not agree with him. He saw the temperatures I had and knew how often I had them.

Suffering an invisible chronic illness not only makes doctors, and others, but you also, begin to question your own judgment. After a doctor tells you a mental evaluation is in order, suddenly the thought that you might be a hypochondriac, or mentally ill, seems too close to real. I recall crying and telling Dr. Bercher, after the doctor in Dallas had said I needed a mental evaluation, "If this is in my head, tell me and *I will get it out.*" He assured me that my illnesses were not in my head. He said something was wrong somewhere and suggested that he felt it had something to do with my immune system. That was why he had referred me to an endocrinologist. Indeed, when one has liver disease, the immune system is compromised. When I saw the endocrinologist HCV had not been identified as a disease. If it had been I might still go in and raise my shirt to the doctor as proof I was indeed ill even if it meant being hauled away in a straightjacket.

Over the years, I have said to James, "It's like I never got over that mono thing." In reality, I had not, but it would be twenty-four more years of unexplained illnesses before I would find out.

Barba Covington McCarty

7. Hepatitis B and Hepatitis C (HBV and HCV)

... many are sick and weak among you...
I Corinthians 11:30

V iruses are the smallest known form of life, and HCV is an especially small virus. In spite of the small size, it is extremely aggressive. It weakens the immune system, and the diseased cells multiply and take over.

Viral hepatitis means inflammation of the liver. Several different viruses cause it. There's an alphabet of hepatitis viruses, HAV, HBV, HCV, HDV, HEV and HGV. The two I have been afflicted with, and the two that may result in the need for transplantation are HBV and HCV so I will elaborate only on those two.

* * *

Hepatitis C (HCV)

Hepatitis C is such a sneaky, quiet, epidemic, a reptilian illness for which there is no cure-all elixir. There is only healing that involves the brain, body and spirit together in unison to cope with the illness. Approximately 85 percent of people with HCV develop a chronic form of the disease, 15 percent develop cirrhosis and 5 percent die from liver cancer or cirrhosis caused by the disease. It is a blood-borne disease that just fifteen years ago medical science was unaware of. Acute hepatitis is the initial infection of the disease. If the disease goes untreated and lasts in the blood for more than six months, it is then chronic HCV and starts slow and inevitable damage to the liver. You catch it by coming in contact with infected blood. Transfusions are the cause of most HCV but not all. HCV is a virus that attacks the liver causing inflammation that can lead to cirrhosis, liver cancer and liver failure—all three can be fatal. Unlike other forms of hepatitis, HCV is hard for the immune system to overcome. The incubation period for HCV is two to twenty-five weeks. That means you may be infected and not test positive for up to nearly six months after you contract the disease. It is spread by contact with infected blood—transfusion, needles, razors, body-piercing and tattoo tools—and can be spread from infected mother to her unborn child. Do not share razors, toothbrushes, nail files or clippers, any tool that can have minute amounts of blood on it. Those at risk include health care workers, IV drug users, hemodialysis patients and those with infected sexual partners or multiple sexual partners. It is not widely spread through sexual contact but can happen. My husband and I were together twenty-five years after I had the mononucleosis-type thing, and he tested negative. It is easier spread to females through sexual contact than to males.

The symptoms, if they are present, are the same as with HBV. There is treatment for HCV now with Interferon and combination therapies with varying success. It is very important to get treatment as soon as possible; early treatment is the reason for successful treatment. Still, even with early treatment, successful treatment happens only 30 to 40 percent of the time; fortunately, nowadays with treatment there is that 30 to 40 percent chance of stopping or slowing the disease's progression with medication therapy and lifestyle changes. Once diagnosed, the progression of the disease depends on how you take care of your health. Doctors have repeatedly told me that my lifestyle is why I am alive today and why my liver, damaged as it was, lasted as long as it did after chronic infection of HCV. Possibly my lifestyle also made my illness last longer. But, since a test for HCV was not developed until 1992, had I not had the lifestyle I do, I might not have been around at all for a transplant.

In a world of invisible chronic illness, I lost confidence, was drained of self-worthiness and became a different person than I was before. An invisible chronic illness has a significant impact on how one feels about his or herself. The illness enters your psychological being as well as your physical being and is devastating. As the illness progressed, there was a profound sadness that encompassed me, since I could no longer do the activities I once enjoyed. I was struggling far too hard to stay alive to have thoughts of taking my own life but there are people with HCV that do contemplate suicide. As the disease progressed, I had difficulty concentrating and was absentminded. Insomnia was a major problem for me. I went days with only a few hours sleep. I could have attended a support group had there been one in my area when I was first diagnosed, but later I could not have gone to one at anytime or anywhere as the disease worsened and I became weaker. However, when I was first diagnosed I would not have gone even if there had been a group available in my area. I didn't want people watching for symptoms and feeling sorry for me. And, I certainly was not going to moan and groan to a room full of strangers; I didn't even tell the people closest to me when I was sick until I got to have-to-go-to-bed-sick. I thought that group meetings were nothing more than pity parties, and I wanted no part of them. After I was diagnosed, I signed in and eavesdropped on fellow diseased people's conversations on the online support groups, but I did not participate. I am a figure-it-out-myself kind of person. I have since changed my mind about that; the best help for a person with HCV is someone else who has tread the road before you and can tell you that you are normal and the problem is not you the problem is the disease. The really great teachers come from the hepatitis C and/or transplant world. For me that was one-on-one, for others it may be in a group setting.

It was determined that I had once had double trouble, hepatitis B and hepatitis C. I had recovered from HBV but not from the lion that ruled my life for so long, HCV.

If you had a blood transfusion before July 1992, you have an increased risk of having been infected with HCV. Hemodialysis patients are a high-risk group. Intravenous drug users and people who have had multiple sexual partners are at high-risk for the disease. It can be passed from a pregnant woman to her unborn child.

If you test positive, your doctor will determine if you have liver disease and refer you to a specialist, a hepatologist, a liver disease specialist, if at all possible.

If you have been diagnosed with a liver disease and you retain nothing else from this book retain the next sentence. *See a hepatologist.* A hepatologist is a doctor who has special training for treatment of liver diseases. Hepatology is a rapidly changing field with new viruses and new treatments for them. To get the highest level of care for your liver disease seek out and find a hepatologist. Many are in large cities affiliated with university-based hospitals that have a liver transplant program and hepatobiliary surgeons.

If a hepatologist is not close enough to your area, or for some reason you cannot get to a hepatologist then, by all means, see a gastroenterologist, a specialist who treats diseases of the stomach, intestines and liver.

If your doctor does not provide you with a referral, ask for one. A general practitioner cannot be expected to be current on the treatment of HCV. HCV is a complicated disease with treatment constantly changing. You must develop an assertive attitude toward your disease.

Approximately 85 percent of those chronically infected with HCV develop liver disease that causes cirrhosis in 50 percent of the cases. Many never know they have HCV until years later when symptoms of cirrhosis appear. For some there are symptoms of flu-like illness, and for others the only symptoms may be jaundice, build up of bile that causes the skin and eyes to go yellow, however, most individuals with viral hepatitis do not experience jaundice. Some will have mild fever, muscle or joint aches, vague abdominal pain and diarrhea. Many have symptoms so unnoticeable they do not realize they are infected. With all that is known about the viruses that cause hepatitis, many who have liver disease are unaware of how they contracted the initial virus and many are unaware they even had the initial virus.

Testing was not available when I had initial HBV and HCV but now it is. There are accurate tests to detect the virus but not tests to determine the levels of the virus in your system.

An ALT test measures the amount of an enzyme "alanine aminotransferase" (ALT) in the blood. An elevated ALT means there is liver inflammation but it doesn't reveal the cause of the inflammation. Further testing is needed to reveal the cause of liver inflammation.

There is no vaccination and no cure for HCV, hepatitis C. It is primarily spread through infected blood. It can be transmitted through contaminated needles used for IV drugs, tattooing and body piercing. Do not share personal items like razors, toothbrushes or nail files or nail clippers that might have minute amounts of blood on them. I am aware I am repeating this sentence. *I am repeating so it is not forgotten.*

Over five million Americans have HBV or HCV, resulting in thirteen thousand to fifteen thousand deaths annually.

The liver is a complex organ that provides hundreds of functions. It can be thought of as the body's refinery. Your liver helps you by producing quick energy when it is needed, manufacturing new body proteins, preventing shortages of body fuel by storing certain vitamins, minerals and sugars, regulating transport of fat stores, regulating blood clotting, producing bile to aid in the digestion process, controlling the production and the excretion of cholesterol, neutralizing and destroying poisonous substances, metabolizing alcohol, maintaining hormone balance, storing iron, regenerating its own damaged tissue, helping the body resist infection by producing immune factors and by removing bacteria from the blood stream and by serving as the main organ of blood formation before birth. With all that it does there are still many other functions of the liver.

There are many types of liver disease with varying signs and symptoms such as fatigue or loss of stamina, abnormally yellow discoloration of the skin and eyes, dark urine, light-colored stools, nausea, vomiting, loss of appetite, vomiting of blood, abdominal swelling from fluid accumulating in the abdominal cavity, prolonged generalized itching, sleep disturbances, mental confusion and coma for patients with severe liver disease.

I am a blond and very fair skinned. I had observed, and so had relatives and friends, that I had blood vessels close to the surface on my face. I never went out without makeup but when overnight relatives or friends did happen to see me without it they would say things like, "You've got measles," or "What happened to your face?" I would always tell them it was surface veins. I did not know it but they were spider veins caused by hormonal imbalance due to liver disease. For as long as I can remember in my adult life, I had a purplish place on the right side of my neck. Friends and family asked and teased me often and repeatedly about the spot being a hickey. Since the transplant I no longer have my measles or my hickey. I had dry eyes for years and treated them with Duratears and all the other artificial tears products on the market. Even though I did not know it then, the spider veins on my face and neck, arthritis-type aches and pains and dry eyes were all signs of liver disease; they were the only visible signs of a disease that I had no idea I had. Later, when the disease was more advanced, if I barely bumped or scratched my arms or hands, they would bleed or get purple patches on them. These were the visible signs of advanced liver disease that I had until I was well past the beginning of end-stage liver disease when I became emaciated with dark circles under my eyes, sunken cheeks and jaundice.

HCV progresses at a slow pace and may be undetected in one's system, as in my case, for decades. It is a 24/7 struggle. It took my life away and was a factor in the breakup of my marriage. I do not offer this as an excuse for my husband. Yes, the vows are 'til death do us part' not 'til you get ill and I can't take it' but it still affects a marriage. The chronic illness of HCV is a family illness. If affects everybody in the family. Since we had no children, for me family was my husband and me.

* * *

Hepatitis B (HBV)

Hepatitis B, HBV, is acquired from transfusions or other blood products with an incubation period of six to twenty-three weeks. Transmission of HBV is much easier than for HCV. It can be transmitted through minute cuts or abrasions or by such simple acts as tooth brushing, ear piercing and tattooing and having dental work done or by sexual contact in seminal fluid, vaginal secretions, even a human bite. It can be transmitted from a pregnant woman to her unborn child. Those having sex with an infected person are at risk as well as those with multiple sexual partners or those engaging in oral or anal sexual practices. Injection drug users are at high risk as are health care workers. There may be no symptoms, and some people may experience mild flu-like symptoms, light-colored stools, dark urine, jaundice, fatigue and fever. Unlike HCV, there is a vaccine for HBV, given in three separate doses, that lasts for years.

If your family immigrated from Africa, Southeast Asia, Mediterranean countries, or the Caribbean, where hepatitis B affects up to 15 percent of the population, you should have a blood test to determine if you are a carrier. If any member of your family or a sexual partner tests positive for HBV, ask your doctor to test you for the virus. If the test is negative, your doctor will vaccinate you against the virus.

According to the American Liver Foundation, if you were stuck with a needle used by a person with AIDS, you'd have a one in two thousand chance of picking up the AIDS virus. But, if that person had hepatitis B, your chance of picking up the HBV increases to one in four! Never, ever, touch a discarded syringe or needle.

Barba Covington McCarty

8. Family Matters

And if one member suffers, all the members suffer with it...
I Corinthians 12:26

My parents had four children, then after twelve years, they had me. An accident. They liked me so well, or each other possibly, that they had another accident fifteen months later, so I am the oldest accident. My mother died of heart disease when I was twelve and my little sister, Beverly, was eleven. To the older four siblings, Beverly and I are the babies of the family. This always bugged me greatly. I didn't mind being one of "the girls" but I did mind being one of "the babies." However, in our close, private world where Beverly and I were the surviving children of Mama's death, I have assumed the self-imposed position of the big sister. Beverly never minded; she loves being the baby. I am in a rather unique birth order position; I am one of the babies and the oldest child all rolled into one package of confusion within the family. But, then so is my sister Betty who is the baby of the first litter but was thrust into the role of dealing with my difficult father and—though she was married with a small son of her own and lived forty miles away—seeing after Bev and me after Mama's death. Betty was the one we called on to resolve any problems, and when girls are eleven and twelve years old, there are many problems. She was always there. It's easy to see why she is still the worrier over Bev and me after years of fussing over us as though we were her cubs.

Nonetheless, I have first child syndrome and am always in control and right bossy at times.

I informed my family of my illness. The response from my sisters, Betty, who still lives forty miles away and Beverly, who lives sixty miles away was one of concern but it is the nature of both of them not to want details. They seemed to be of the opinion that if they didn't acknowledge the illness then it didn't exist. And, after all, I had been sick with something or other for over twenty years. In reality they had no idea how often I was sick. They had no idea that on my best day I was sick, no one did, not even my husband or my doctor.

I did not inform them of my decision not to take Interferon and had no fear that they would find out about it and insist I take it, as neither of them is inquisitive about such matters even when it is their own illnesses. I was back in charge.

Barba Covington McCarty

9. Progression – Moving Backwards

Look up and not down;
Look forward and not back;
Look out and not in...
The Lend a Hand Society Motto by Edward Everett Hale, 1871

L iver disease is a different course for everyone, before surgery and afterwards. Chronic illness does not check your calendar. It makes you live in the now with no past and no future. As hard and as long as I fought, I finally accepted it only because I had no other choice.

End-stage liver disease ran my life for many, many years. My whole life. It dictated what I did for fun and when I did what I had to do out of necessity. Also, out of necessity, everything had to be easy. Later, even necessities were so controlled by the disease that they were left undone. But, still when someone asked, "How are you?" my reply was, "I'm just great." I craved normalcy.

End-stage liver disease is defined as liver disease that has caused the quality of life to deteriorate to an unacceptable level with the patient's inability to perform usual activities such as work or caring for the family or home. Even with that definition, that I am aware of now but I was not aware of at the time, it is still difficult to pinpoint when end-stage liver disease began. Back when I was diagnosed it was hard to adjust to the pain of knowing and adapt to a new world even less alive than the slowed-down world I had lived in for so many years already. I had already quit work two years earlier and had held on for several more years while I was unable to work but refused to quit. I had been in a state of end-stage liver disease for a long time before I had my gallbladder removed and liver disease was discovered.

I should have pressed for a referral earlier that would have gotten me on the waiting list earlier. Instead I waited while I tried to prove to myself that I did not have to give up. My desire to tough it out made the diagnosis come later than it might have. Still I was luckier than many people with the disease so well advanced. When I did press the issue with my doctor, I was referred to Baylor University Medical Center (BUMC).

As my disease progressed, visits to Dr. Weinstein were more frequent for dietary counseling, diuretic therapy and correction of fluid and electrolyte imbalances.

Our livers are filters for the blood stream and are designed to last a lifetime. The liver's very function damages it. Because of their designated job when we are born, our livers begin degeneration.

Modern society has added to the livers' workload and liver diseases are on the increase. Part of the increase may be due to our frequent contact with chemicals and environmental pollutants. Toxins lurk in medicines, food additives and air pollutants and many of those are impossible to avoid completely. However, you can give your liver a little extra help. Whenever you are nursing a compromised liver, as those with hepatitis are, it is important to give it as much help as possible by reducing the toxins that come in contact with your body. Even without HCV the liver can use the help.

Just think how many times a day we use aerosol sprays; deodorant, hair spray, room fresheners, cleansers, bug sprays, paint and many others.

In spite of warnings many years ago, many of us still have our clothing dry-cleaned with perchloroethylene, a solvent used in dry cleaning.

The amount of medicine consumed has greatly increased and so has dangers to the liver. How many times do we use over-the-counter medications for a touch of a headache or another pain that is minimal, a slightly stuffy nose or other minor afflictions?

The FDA does not regulate nutritional supplements, so purity, source and strength of available products vary widely. Herbal remedies fall into the category of non-regulated supplements and many are harmful to our livers and other organs as well. For some health food junkies, vitamin overuse is the problem; vitamin A in doses exceeding 25,000 international units per day can cause severe liver damage. Niacin is another that can cause liver damage if excessive doses are taken. Most medications are harmful to our livers. Read the labels.

Think how often we mix medicines without our doctor's advice. Many people have taken over-the-counter drugs and drank beer, liquor or wine. Many people have drank alcohol with prescribed medications without consulting their doctor. Many people drink more than two alcoholic drinks per day.

How many of us have gone on a cleaning binge and used aerosol cleansers without proper ventilation? In my very young days, I remember using a cleaning mixture of Clorox bleach and Comet cleanser and almost passing out from the fumes. But it cleaned the bathtub like nothing else.

Have you ever spread fertilizers and insecticides without the proper protection? Your liver knows.

Work places are riddled with pollutants that are hazardous to our health. High levels of chronic liver disease have been reported in refrigeration engineers, dry cleaners, people who work in the agriculture industry, hair dressers and nail technicians, industrial chemists, rubber manufacturers and people who work in the automotive, plumbing and building industries.

Everything we eat, drink, breathe or put on our skin goes through the liver so everyday life taxes our livers. Filtering every day life is the liver's job but an overload of work for it can mean earlier or sudden death to us.

Added taxes on some livers include use of street drugs in any form, needles, sniffing or huffing. The liver is the brunt of many jokes about alcohol. There are many people recovering from transplants that will tell you when you have drunk enough alcohol to have cirrhosis the buzz is gone along with the jokes.

Experts estimate that more than half of all liver disease could be prevented if people acted upon the knowledge we have already gained from research.

In spite of everything I did to stop or slow down my disease, it progressed anyway by my liver just doing its job. With the exception of Clorox and Comet cleaning mixture that I quit using years ago, I have always been careful of aerosols and pollutants. How much sooner would it have progressed had I been careless with modern society's pollutants?

I refrained from using or being near anyone who sprayed aerosols. When I had gasoline pumped, or pumped it myself, I rolled the car window up to avoid smelling the fumes or stood on the side of the pump where the wind blew the gasoline fumes the other way. I used liquid cleansers for cleaning my house and ventilated well when I used them. My allergic reactions to medications continued to mount, so I avoided, as I had for several years, taking even over-the-counter medications unless absolutely necessary. A scarred liver's filtering process is slow, therefore, the concentration of what the liver filters is greater, so allergic reactions occur.

I tired so fast that I only went to the food store when absolutely necessary. I had my home delivery newspaper stopped, because I could no longer go to the front yard, about ten feet from my garage, to get it. The good thing about having to force myself to eat and not eating as much was that I didn't have to struggle through the food store as often. I have left a food cart with items in it many times, because I could not make it through the food store. For years, I went to WalMart late at night, after 11 PM or midnight because I could park closer and the store wasn't as crowded. Shopping during regular hours slowed me down and made me waste the little energy I had by standing in lines. Later, because of its size and the size of the parking lot and crowds there, going to Wal-Mart was totally out of the question. As my disease progressed, by the time I parked the car and got inside the front doors I was exhausted. I have sat on the benches located between the front doors of Wal-Mart more than a few times just so I could make it back to the car without ever having gone inside the store; because I was too fatigued just from walking from the car to the bench to do the job I had come to do. It was totally unacceptable for me to use the motorized carts, they are for handicapped people—and even if I had the energy to learn to use them; getting in and out of them would have used more energy than pushing the cart that I held onto for steadiness. During the early years of my disease, I devised alternate routes of travel that had the least amount of traffic and traffic stops because the time and energy I used on the road was energy I needed when I got to where I was going.

There was no such thing as getting a shower, getting dressed then going to the doctor. I made just-after-noon appointments so I could shower early in the morning and go back to bed and rest a couple of hours. After two hours or so of rest, I could get up, get dressed and sit in the recliner and rest until appointment time. I went to the appointments early so I wouldn't be to crying-stage tired from walking from the parking lot to the exam room. I needed the time to rest in the waiting room after the walk from the car and before the walk to the exam room to see the doctor.

I didn't even have the energy to pick up a small child. My stream was dry; it no longer ran into the river of life and living.

Nosebleeds became an event multiple times during a day. I awoke to nosebleeds on many occasions and would have blood on my pillowcase until morning because I did not have the energy to get up and change the pillowcase. Since my transplant, I no longer have to use the plastic covers like some hotels and hospitals have that making crinkling noises when I turn my head on the pillows.

Spider veins that look like small varicose veins are common for HCV patients and were on my face years before they began to be on my chest and shoulders.

The first time Dr. Weinstein removed a yield of twenty-one liters of fluid from my belly, a procedure called paracentesis, I would have sworn he was coming at me with a spear. So... I never looked again. However, my friend, Mary, watched as though she was taking lessons and teased me as she watched my second paracentesis by saying she could do it next time at home. Having never been pregnant, I don't know, but all my friends who felt my belly afterwards, at Mary's suggestion, said that it felt like a post delivery belly feels. After each paracentesis, I left Dr. Weinstein's office holding my pants up. I finally learned and brought smaller pants to wear home.

I was determined to live. I had a will to live. I had strength to live. I had a positive attitude. The key to surviving the time between end-stage liver disease and transplant is positive attitude. If you think you are beaten, you are. I knew I could do it. No matter how sick I got, I never, ever once thought of giving up. I kept a gratitude journal (Thank you for the idea, Oprah.) to help me keep a positive attitude. On my list of things to do, live was #1.

I cannot stress enough the value of humor therapy; laugh as though you are not ill for as long as you can. What can you lose by laughing? A serious disease deserves serious laughter. I did the "Quivered Liver Reports" to my email friends and family, and in fact, my email address was quiveredliver@yahoo.com. I have since cancelled that email address, as it no longer applies. When medical expenses came up, I made comments about livers being expensive pieces of meat and even then it was only good with onions. And, when I became permanently (it seemed) jaundiced, I said I never did look good in yellow. Reader's Digest is correct, "Laughter is the Best Medicine."

* * *

I am better now but there are people out there still walking in my old boots, so I would like to address those family and friends in the spirit of wanting to be informed and who mean so well but have never experienced chronic hepatitis C.

Please understand that most of the day is spent in exhaustion, not tiredness, exhaustion accompanied by weakness. Please know that "I am exhausted" does "not" mean I am asleep and do not want company. It simply means I am exhausted and may not be as much fun as I used to be. I have been sick for years and cannot go around miserable for years like one can with a bad case of the flu. Feeling sick is a way of life for me.

When I laugh and you tell me I "sound" good does not mean I am better, it means I am still a happy person and even if I am deathly ill and in pain I still need to laugh. When I miss a call and you tell my answering machine that I must be better since I am out running around, please note if I am not at the doctor, I may be sitting in the parking lot somewhere crying, or praying or wishing, I could get the stamina to finish the job I started. Please do not assume that since you saw me out shopping in the morning that I am all right that afternoon or the next day. Most likely, because I made that short trip in the morning I am not feeling well. Because hepatitis C is variable, I may be able to go shopping today but not be able to go down the hallway to my kitchen or to get my newspaper from the yard the next.

Please don't tell me that "everything's gonna be all right" and remind me I am not normal; I know everything is not all right. Tell me, "I'm here for you," then be there for me.

Telling me to get out and do things does not make me feel like getting out and doing things; my doctor and I are running the show, such as it is, and I know when I can get out and do things and when I have pushed my body to its limit.

Please know that I have to rest before I do things to be able to endure what I do. Ask me to go places, sometimes I do feel like it. When you ask me to do something, ask me if I feel like going to a movie instead of asking me how I feel then assuming I don't feel like going. I may feel like going to a movie but not a trip to a restaurant or vice versa. It may largely depend on the walk. And, when I do go shopping with you, please don't get lost from me in the store so I have to use up my precious energy looking for you.

Although I may not seem enthusiastic, I still want to hear about your life, job and kids, even your grandkids.

Please don't ask me if I "need anything" assume I do and volunteer with "I'm here to vacuum," "I'm going to Kroger; what do you need?" or "I'm coming to take you to the doctor." If I can do chores or run errands, I will not abuse your generous offer because it is important to me that I feel like I can do things for myself when I can.

I do want visitors. Visits are much more personal and lasting than a call; however I do want you to call me too.

I need you to understand that these suggestions, that may appear to be rules, but are not, may change drastically as I get into end-stage liver disease when I am rarely able to be out at all. You are my link to the outside world that this disease has removed me from. You are dear to me, and I depend on you.

And... other people's cooking tastes so good.

10. The Liver Transplant Team

He shall give his angels charge over thee to keep thee in all thy ways. They
shall bear thee up in their hands lest thou dash thy foot against a stone.
Psalms 91:11-12

When I was hospitalized, I saw different members of the transplant team daily. There is a reason for that, if a surgeon is involved with the surgical procedure to obtain organs for donation or is transplanting them into recipient patients he is elsewhere and won't be doing rounds, so obviously, there is a rotation process that must be done. Record keeping at Baylor is exceptional, and the day's doctor who makes the rounds is informed of your condition and its complications if they are present.

There are many more doctors than those listed below who treated me at Baylor, in fact there are too many to mention. Others I remember include Harry Sarles, JR, MD who performed many angiograms; Robert M. Goldstein, MD, FACS who performed a stent procedure; and Norman G. Diamond, MD who I saw regularly in the Interventional Radiology Department. There are others who treated me that I am positive I am forgetting, some I have no recollection of their names but I remember their special care. I especially remember a kidney specialist and a neurosurgeon but not their names. The doctors who played a major part in me living today are listed in detail below. There is no other word for these men. They are angels all.

Jeffrey Weinstein, MD kept me alive until a B positive donor liver was donated for me. I read Elizabeth Parr's book, *I'm Glad Your Not Dead*, which I found and ordered online. In the book Parr stresses finding a good hepatologist, a liver specialist. So, I called Dr. Weinstein's office and asked if he was a hepatologist. He is a hepatologist and specializes in gastroenterology at Baylor University Medical Center. He was, indeed, just what I needed. He was educated at University of Texas Southwestern School of Allied Health and did his internship at UT affiliated hospitals. His fellowship was at Mayo Clinic. Jeffrey Weinstein has boyish good looks. He is professional, very pleasant, but not chatty. He wears the smallest pair of jeans I have ever seen make rounds on 14 Roberts on Saturday. He is easily young enough to be my son. I do not recall a specific reason why, but when I first met him, I was not comfortable with him. My prayer in my journal on July 25, 2000, for Dr. Weinstein reads: "Dear God, Grant Dr. Weinstein the wisdom to be comfortable not only with his medical knowledge and expertise but to also make the good doctor person inside him a great doctor person by leaving off trying to prove himself. He has the potential for greatness with compassion. You are a wonderful God and can handle this one problem in his life. Amen."

It worked. From the next visit on I was comfortable. I suspect Dr. Weinstein did not change; I have a strong suspicion I did. I was not going to die. I was determined to live. And, Dr. Weinstein made me feel certain that my outcome would be good. I have no idea what he had done to make me think he was trying to prove himself when I wrote that prayer, possibly encephalopathy at work. He has certainly proven himself to me.

I got online and discovered Baylor UMC had the best facility for liver transplantation in the country; the stats online that showed how many successful transplants done there prove it to me.

Goran Klintmalm, PhD, FACS, the director of Baylor's transplantation department, was always articulate, professional and formal until very near the end of my stay at Baylor when he became informal. Again, I suspect I was the one who changed when I felt better and became my normal yapping self again after much speech therapy. He did my second surgery when I had a "kink" that had to be repaired.

Dr. Klintmalm received his Doctor of Medicine and his PhD degrees at the Karolinska Institute, Stockholm, Sweden, where he did his internship, residency and fellowship. His fellowship in transplantation surgery was done at the University of Colorado, Denver, and at the University of Pittsburg under Thomas Starzi, MD, a major international pioneer in the field of transplant surgery. Dr. Starzi performed the first liver transplant in the world in 1967. Dr. Klintmalm was recruited in 1984 to start the liver transplant program at Baylor. He is author and co-author of more than 340 publications, and together with Dr. Ronald Busuttil, he is the author of the prevailing textbook in liver transplantation titled, *Transplantation of the Liver,* the bible of liver transplantation. Dr. Klintmalm has served as councilor of United Network for Organ Sharing (UNOS) region 4, as well as being a member of the UNOS board. He is past president of the Texas Transplant Society, and he served as councilor of the American Society of Transplant Surgeons. And, that is why Baylor University Medical Center is the world-class liver transplant program that it is.

Marlon F. Levy, MD, FACS, the then assistant director of Transplantation Services at BUMC, is chatty and informal but very articulate. Dr. Levy enters the room already speaking while pushing the door open saying, "How are you, Honey?" He was educated at University of Texas Southwestern Medical School in Dallas, Texas, and served his residency and internship at the Medical College of Wisconsin. He did his fellowship at BUMC Children's Memorial Medical Center, Chicago. He completed his transplant surgery fellowship at BUMC in Dallas. He is also medical director of Southwest Transplant Alliance, the organ procurement agency in the area of Texas where I live. He has a major research interest in xenotransplantation, the potential application of animal organs to meet the need for human organs in transplantation. Dr. Levy is the surgeon who kept a young man alive with xeno profusion, a genetically modified pig's liver and a machine, until a liver could be found for the desperately ill young man. Xeno profusion is a process by which a patient's blood is taken from the leg through a pump where it is heated and oxygenated. Then the blood is filtered and returned to the patient's liver. Behind Dr. Levy's desk is a giant-sized black and white photo of the young man while he was hospitalized at BUMC connected to the xeno profusion machine. His office is filled with pigs, stuffed pigs, statues and pictures of pigs.

Much research is being done to further transplantation. Other than xeno profusion, which keeps a person awaiting a liver transplant alive until a human liver is obtained, there is a machine called a bio artificial liver with a process similar to kidney dialysis that detoxifies the liver with the help of cells from pig's livers. Some patients have recovered and been removed from transplant waiting lists after treatment with the machine. For other patients, the treatment has been used as a bridge for severely ill patients awaiting liver transplants.

The ultimate goal is to use genetically modified pigs livers for transplantation as another source of organs to eliminate the many deaths that occur because of the lack of human donor livers.

Dr. Levy's knowledge and commitment have taken him elsewhere since my transplant. He is now the medical director of the liver/kidney transplant program at Baylor All Saints Medical Center in Ft. Worth, Texas.

Ernesto P. Molmenti, MD, did my transplant surgery. He is informal, articulate and professional. He is a big man; tall and big, but not overweight, the gentle teddy bear type with boyish good looks, a great smile and a beautiful Argentinean accent although he has been in the US since the age of fifteen. I have no doubt he is the subject of many nurses' dreams. He graduated from Boston University School of Medicine and trained in general surgery at Barnes Hospital, Washington School of Medicine in St. Louis, Missouri. He did his transplant training at the University of Pittsburg at the Thomas Starzi Transplantation Institute. Dr. Molmenti is no longer at BUMC. His expertise has taken him elsewhere; he is now the surgical director of the kidney/pancreas transplant program at Johns Hopkins University Hospital in Baltimore, Maryland. He has published extensively and has received numerous awards. When I called his office in Baltimore to get an updated bio for this book he returned my call personally. It was good to hear his voice.

11. Mind Matters

*It is therefore necessary that memorable things should be committed to
writing, ...and not wholly committed to slippery memory, which seldom yields
a certain reckoning.*
Sir Edward Coke, 1660,
Les Reports de Edward Coke, vol. 1

Lactulose acts as a laxative and removes toxins from your body when
your liver can't. As horrible as it is, lactulose is a must for patients
with liver disease, and I was taking it. I knew it was used to remove
toxins from my body. I did not know those toxins if not removed caused
encephalopathy, liver-caused mental impairment, where lack of concentration,
personality changes and temporary loss of memory occur. Neither had I been
told that I was experiencing encephalopathy, possibly a good thing. With the
worst part of my disease set against the backdrop of my marital split, I was a
step away from reality anyway, and encephalopathy was not an area of
research of my disease that I wanted to explore. Encephalopathy was my big
denial with liver disease. I was not open to letting myself think my thinking
was off, let alone someone else thinking it was off.

I am a most organized person. I was organized and organizing everyone
else who would let me years before we heard of Martha Stewart.

There was a time when I could remember a telephone number that I had
heard or seen only once months before.

In the summer of 2000, I began having trouble with figures and
balancing my checkbook. As good as I am at organizing, I am the complete
opposite with mathematics, so having difficulty balancing my checkbook was
no big deal. I am one who keeps my checkbook balanced this way; if I write a
check for $9.99, I deduct $10.00. If I write a check for $9.01, I deduct $10.00.
That way I am never overdrawn, and at the time the bank statement arrives, I
check it and straighten it all out. Close enough is good enough for my
checkbook.

I was a person who never forgot a name, but during my illness I began
forgetting names, sometimes of people I had known a long time. I found
myself losing my train of thought in the middle of a sentence or searching for
my next word. I would pause and often another person supplied the word or
name I was searching for. And, I was on lactulose! Lots of it.

I had lost my body and life, now my mind was skipping out too. I
appeared to myself to be some kind of borderline unorganized fool with yet

another problem that fell into my ever-growing file of "Things I Can Do Nothing About." Even with encephalopathy, I expected more of myself than was realistic at that point, but confidence and self-esteem drown in this illness. I did not know that my mental faculties would be restored along with my health after transplant so I worried over losing my brainpower.

The process of encephalopathy frustrated me greatly and was my greatest cause of anxiety. I was quick and it bothered me not to recall who or what someone was talking about. When I forgot a word or a train of thought, I brought the fact up to a few friends. Every one of them helped me by saying, "it's old age" or "I do it too." But it wasn't normal for me and I knew it. I knew it was encephalopathy, but I didn't tell any of them. I explained it by saying "well that went out my window" when it would happen.

After a visit to Dr. Weinstein during the summer of 2000 my sister, Beverly, who can't possibly share brain cells with me, brought it to my attention this way: "I'm worried about you. I wonder if your thinking is right." While I searched for the words to defend myself—another clue was that I had to search for words—she continued with, "You're not the same; you're acting like me, forgetting things and stuff." We laughed while I continued to search for an explanation that would assure she would not be insisting I go stay with her and get Betty in on it too. She was right I was but I did not admit it. I said that I had talked to Dr. Bercher about it and he said I was fine; that a lot of stuff had happened to me in the last seven years. I talked her out of it; I was still that good!

My good and dear friend Fay delighted in my forgetting things and teased me about it. After awhile, I became irritated with her when she teased me. She had no idea why I was forgetting; I did but I never told her. She knows only now how aggravated it made me when she teased me.

I thought if I knew I was having trouble with the thought process and no one else noticed it then everything was fine.

Encephalopathy for me was quite like summer rain showers; it came and went often, was not unpleasant and everything around me changed for a while.

Encephalopathy had begun, and it was never quite gone from me again until post transplant. It was a cause of alarm for me but since I was still functioning and could do so at my own speed, since I was no longer employed, I dared not tell a soul. And, after I talked Bev out of it not another soul noticed. I was still in control, but I was frustrated and anxious; something else I never told anyone. I was getting sicker and sicker.

12. Liver Buddies

Then an angel from heaven appeared to Him, strengthening Him…
Luke 22:43

I was not a group meeting person, even if there had been one available in my area, so I sought out to talk to others one-on-one who had been transplanted. The best information a person waiting for a transplant can have is from someone who has already had a transplant, preferably, for information sake, one with a gift of gab.

As I became sicker and sicker my friend Darlyn kept telling me I needed to talk to her friend Joanna's mother. For a much longer time, my sister-in-law Clara had been telling me about Mrs. Jones who lived in her community and how bad her liver disease had gotten. She told me about Mrs. Jones lung complications and when she started having to take oxygen with her everywhere. She called me when Mrs. Jones got her transplant and gave me updates on her condition. A year or so later, Darlyn gave me Joanna's mother's telephone number and I called her. I asked her if I could come and visit and ask her questions. She gave me directions to her home in the community where my sister-in-law lived. I did not know it but Darlyn's Joanna's mother was my sister-in-law's Mrs. Jones.

At the time I met Ruth Ann Jones, I had met only one other person who had been the recipient of a liver transplant. I met him when I had just found out I had liver disease. The fact that I had done minimal research when I met him coupled with the fact that he told me only the terrible things about transplant scared me. I was terrified. He was not a doomsday kind of guy; in fact he was a lighthearted-type and told his stories with great comedy. He showed me his scar that seemed to go on forever. After our visit, I didn't say it, but I was as scared as if he had cut me open and sewed me up. I have since decided it was just too soon after I learned that I was going to be in need of a transplant that I met him through a mutual friend. At the time we met, my mind was shifting between my marital breakup and my illness and the seriousness of both.

When I met Ruth Ann, the time was right. I had become accustomed to the fact that I was, if I was lucky and blessed, going to receive a liver transplant. Ruth Ann is not one to volunteer a lot of information, but she emphasized the positives about how she felt afterwards. When I saw her the first time, I could not believe she had undergone a transplant because she looked so healthy. She showed me her Mercedes scar (called so because the scar is an inverted Y.) I was no longer scared by the approximately twenty inches of scar all over her belly.

Later, as I researched further and became sicker and knew what to ask, I called her and asked questions. If she didn't know the answer to my questions, she could tell me where to find the answer. I could ask her anything and I did, except about encephalopathy. She made me feel renewed and I wasn't yet.

Darlyn's Joanna's mother, Clara's Mrs. Jones, my liver buddy, Ruth Ann Jones, another angel.

13. Pre-Transplant Evaluation Week

But an angel of the Lord opened the doors...
Acts 5:19

Baylor has a thorough, rigid and precise screening process that determines the extent of your liver disease through extensive lab tests, X-ray studies and consultations. It is determined through testing that there is no reasonable alternative treatment for the patient's liver disease.

The screening process carries with it a grand prize, and that grand prize is life. However, getting to that prize was through the door of a grueling pre-transplant evaluation week.

There are reasons a patient may be excluded as a candidate for transplantation. They are: alcohol or other chemical abuse that has not been stopped within six months of consideration, metastatic malignancy or other non-hepatic primary malignancy, serious diseases such as infection, heart or lung disease, history of non-compliance with a previous medical regimen, inadequate family or other support system, HIV-positive status, multiple previous upper abdominal surgeries and advance age; however, certain individuals over the age of sixty may be considered for transplantation depending on their vigor.

Damage to your liver must be severe enough to warrant a transplant, but you must be healthy enough to withstand and survive the procedure. In other words, you must be dying, but you must be picky about what part of you is dying.

My friend, Mary Merritt, went with me and stayed the week of my pre-transplant evaluation. To say pre-transplant evaluation testing is rigid is an understatement. For me pre-transplant evaluation week was one of the worst parts of transplant. I felt pre-evaluation week was the door to the grand prize of life and that door was just outside of hell. I thought I would die, and was wishing I would sometimes, as we traipsed around the huge hospital lost a big part of the time. Baylor UMC is a huge place. Being a stranger to the place meant retracing long corridors just to reach the correct testing place. If we got lost I sat and waited, more than once in the floor crying, while Mary found the correct way and came back for me. The week of testing with all the walking would be tough for someone able to run marathons on weekends but for someone without enough stamina to walk to the yard and pick up the newspaper it is almost impossible. I could not have made it without Mary. She let me out of the car as close to the door as possible everyday, parked the car and located the rooms where tests were to be, then, if needed, wheeled me the long distances in one of the hospital's wheelchairs. I was exhausted everyday before we started on the day's run of tests, and by the end of the day, I was beyond any fatigue I had ever experienced.

The schedule consisted of a CT (CAT) scan, MRI, DISIDA, cholangiogram, sonogram, MUGA scan, skeletal survey, bone scan, electrocardiogram (EEG, EKG) angiogram, echocardiogram, glofil and pulmonary function test and a nutritional evaluation, a test for AIDS and a psychosocial evaluation.

The last associate I saw during pre-transplant evaluation week was the one who collects the specimen for AIDS testing. Before the test, she informed me that if I tested positive for AIDS they would not tell me but that I had to test. I said OK and entered the very small restroom and closed the door behind me. She tapped lightly in the door and said it had to remain open. I, being one who cannot go if I am aware anyone is within hearing distance, asked her why. She said she had to witness that I gave the specimen, that I had not carried a specimen by someone else into the restroom and poured it in the little cup. I managed to squeeze out barely enough for a specimen with Mary outside the door laughing, almost to the point of having Felix spasms.

My kidneys, lungs, heart and pancreas were sound for withstanding transplant. I did well on all the tests except the nutritional evaluation.

It was revealed to me that I was B positive blood type, that's one of the rare ones; 5 percent of the population is AB blood type, 10 percent of the population is B blood, 40 percent is type A and 45 percent is type O.

I sat down before a doctor at the end of the last day of testing, and he said, "I found only one problem... you are malnourished." Being a chubette (that's English for fat) most of my adult life and weighing in during my pre-transplant evaluation week at one hundred eighty pounds I laughed, and said, "Yeah." I could not believe anyone weighing one hundred eighty pounds could be malnourished. I had become emaciated, my face skeletal and temples sunken. I rarely ate and often upchucked if I did, but I still carried one hundred eighty pounds. The fluid associated with ascites was the reason. He explained to me that the visible sign was my sunken temples. Had I noticed? Yes, but I had no idea what it meant. I thought I was just getting sicker, and, of course, my skeletal face showed I was. The doctor, who shall remain nameless, as encephalopathy does not let me recall which doctor it was that day, patted his desk and said to me, "If I had a B-positive liver sitting right here on my desk in a cooler, I could not give it to you today. You have to gain some weight." I thought I had failed the entire pre-evaluation week on this final day, and I thought it was because I needed to gain weight. Had I not been astounded by the news I might have insisted the doctor, whoever he was, call Dr. Bercher, my family practitioner, and tell him that I simply had to gain some weight; that would show him after all those years he insisted, though he did it gently, that I lose weight. The doctor continued and said while I waited for a transplant I would have to drink Ensure, a nutritional supplement drink that supplies calories, vitamins and minerals. He said I had to drink lots of rich-tasting Ensure… that I could not keep down.

I devised a plan to suck it down, as much as I could, all in a hurry. Bad, bad idea. I was scared that I could not keep the thick liquid down, and I would not be able to get the nourishment needed to get a transplant. As far as I know there is not a way to keep down what wants so badly to come up. I went home and tried to drink Ensure and eventually changed to Wal-Mart's equivalent, Equate, in a formula I devised halved with skim milk. Room temp, right out of the can or over ice was a no go. Refrigerated worked best. Most days I managed to drink, and keep down, only half of the prescribed amount of four cans daily.

I was lucky. I did not have to have the endoscopy because of the danger of causing a variceal bleed, bleeding from varicose veins in the food pipe or stomach, due to having portal hypertension. A previous endoscopy showed that I had enlarged veins. Neither did I have to get a biopsy, the removal of a small piece of the liver with a long needle to determine the extent of damage to a liver or to diagnose the type liver disease one has. Biopsies are invasive procedures and are not done without a real need because there is a risk of infection and/or bleeding. Now I know that was to save room for sticks with that long needle after surgery, when I lost count after six liver biopsies. After about the second one, biopsies are as easy as getting blood drawn. I also did not have to have the cardiac first pass and stress test as I strongly believe they were attempting to save my life by not putting me on a stationary bicycle or a treadmill. No, to this day, I do not know what all of the test are; but there are lots of them, all with good reason I'm sure.

I was most worried about having the MRI, because I had experienced two failed attempts at having one in Paris when I developed a migraine, felt I was smothering and escalated to vomiting in their trashcan. I did finally succeed when I absolutely had to have one. I was placed into a huge thing that strongly resembled a concrete grave for about six people. Phyllis and Bobby were up in between the "concrete" with me, talking me through it until I fell asleep from the Valium I'd been prescribed beforehand. Back then, the one in Paris, Texas was considered an open MRI, and the one at Baylor is a closed one where you are pushed through a tunnel. But, the difference was the tunnel had air circulating inside and there was no huge thing of "concrete" coming down on you. I have since had an MRI in the new one at Paris that is much smaller and more open. I didn't have a Valium prescribed, get a migraine, vomit in their trashcan or have anyone else in the machine with me. I wonder also if possibly part of the problem with the first tries in the big machine was due to encephalopathy caused by liver disease. However, I do not intend to try it again to see.

Although it was July, and July in Texas is hot, no exceptions, I was cold even outside. Being cold is one of the symptoms of liver disease. I had been cold for at least twelve years. I wore sweats when Mary and I went out to eat supper, or when Mary went to eat, and I did the usual picking at my food. We did find a Sonic nearby that had just started making a drink of ice cream, ice and cola, called a flurry. I could drink Coke flurries and keep them down. What a deal! If I could have had Ensure in them it would have been great.

At week's end, I tested out as a viable candidate for transplant and was "on the waiting list" by hospital standards, but since my insurance was paying, I would have to wait until my HMO okayed the surgery to be on the list officially.

So, I entered the world of transplant. A world where there are those who make it and those who do not. I knew I could make it through the surgery, but I was not as sure I could make it through the wait.

Once in fear of transplant surgery, I now felt like celebrating it but, as ill as I was, celebrating was far too big of a challenge.

Dr. Jeffrey Weinstein presented my individual case to the liver transplant selection committee that meets at Baylor on Wednesday afternoons. The committee is composed of physicians from various specialties, a transplant social worker and the medical and surgical nurse transplant coordinators. Each case is discussed, and it is determined if the patient is suitable, both medically and psychosocially.

It is crucial to have a clear picture of how one handles stress and who is available to you for emotional support. I was worried about having to explain the availability of a support system, since every time I saw Dr. Weinstein a different friend, sister or niece was with me. Later the doctors, nurses and coordinators commented on the many different people—my angels—who came to my room to stay with me as though it was a good thing. It was. I was lucky.

My husband's company changed insurance carriers right at the time my letter was mailed from Baylor to them for approval. It took the approval seven weeks to arrive in the mail when I began the official long wait for an organ. I anticipated that wait to be at least the average wait of fifteen months maybe longer since my blood type was B positive. Maybe not soon enough. Maybe I wouldn't make it.

B-positive waiting lists are shorter, but the rarity of the blood type also means B-positive donors are fewer, so, the shorter list means nothing. Even with all the different feelings that ran through me, I had more positive thoughts than negative ones. I was sure everything was going to be all right "Whatever all right turned out to be" a saying I picked up years ago from my friend Joann when she had a serious illness of her own. As I sat worried and crying about her illness, to make me feel better, she said, "It's all right. I don't know what all right is yet but it's going to be all right." That saying and thought imprinted in my mind years ago by Joann was possibly the thought that shaped my attitude that got me through my illness and transplant.

My transplant story is specific, as are all liver transplant patients' stories. Liver diseases vary. Even when you have the same disease as someone else, the complications will vary.

December 1999

April 2000

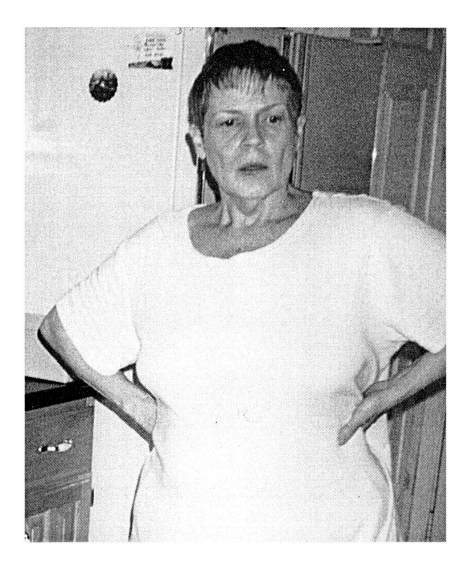

August 2000

Barba Covington McCarty

14. The Patient Patiently Waits

Behold, I send an angel before thee, to keep thee in thy way.
Exodus 23:20

I n the world of transplant the wait for an organ is the only thing that can wait. Everything else in preparation of a transplant cannot wait, as I will talk about later in this book.

The most difficult part of transplant is waiting. Waiting for an organ is a stressful time in a state of constant anticipation. Life is constantly like being twenty years old and driving behind a little, old, gray-haired lady or man going 20 mph with no way to get around them knowing you could be going 30 mph. It's a constant, antsy watch ahead, and some days you're behind a little old lady, who you are sure knows where she is going; she's just going slowly. Other days you are behind a little old man, and you are sure he has no idea where he's going.

My wait was shorter than most, and I can only imagine how tired one gets of that state after a long wait. It is plagued with many unknowns but the wait allows you to come to terms with what is happening to you in this strange new world of transplant. Knowing there is a critical shortage of organs was my main concern and following on its tail was that I might become too disorientated from encephalopathy to care for myself until a liver was donated for me. Most people say they feel a loss of control. I did not. I had been in that limbo one gets in after the breakup of a long-term marriage; I had lost control of my life already. I already felt like I had lost control of my health as well because of all the things I could no longer do, due to my health, for so many years before. Waiting for the organ was a relief to me. I was near the end of feeling bad or near the end period, and which ever it was, I was fine with it. Unless someone has been there, they do not understand that feeling of getting to the point where it is okay to live or die. It comes after a huge ever-expanding file of "Things I Can Do Nothing About." For me it gave me time to reflect and to realize all that I had: God; my mother for twelve years; a little sister to go through the tough years after Mama's death with; a husband who loved me and let me love him for over twenty-nine years; my niece, Destiny, who loved me as much as I loved her and was my friend and confidant even now that she is grown. When I told her I was going to have to have a liver transplant, she told me "You can have mine," knowing full well that it meant she would no longer be alive. At that time split liver living donor transplants had not been done. I also had jobs I had enjoyed working at, children of friends and relatives around me and later their children in my life; a thirst for learning and a chance to quench that thirst. I had had it all at one time or other.

So, I did not sit and wait for the sake of sitting and waiting. I did my thing… I prepared and organized. Some say that it is frustrating to them to have to be reachable twenty-four hours a day. For me, it was not. I was almost always home, because I could do nothing else; so, I was reachable by phone already. If you are able to be about your daily life-as-usual by all means do not put your life on hold and miss important events in your life.

It is impossible to predict how long anyone will be on the waiting list because no one has control when an organ will become available, so being available anytime on any day at any hour of the day or night is a must. There are those who miss transplants because they do not stay in the area and are unreachable. I had come too far to miss the call, and even if I had been able to go somewhere and be unreachable, I wouldn't have done it. Beepers accidentally go off caused by lightning storms, and wrong numbers are dialed causing great frustration for some.

Once a suitable donor is located, the coordinator will notify you. He or she will ask if you are sick; have a cold, are running a temperature or have a kidney infection. Any illness, as small as a cold, the flu or any other infection can prevent you being able to get the transplant. Develop a habit of frequent hand washing. You will need that habit before you get a transplant when your immune system is affected by your liver disease and you are trying to stay well to be available when the call comes and after transplant when you will be even more susceptible to infection caused by the antirejection drugs that must be taken. You will be instructed on where to report to the hospital. The nursing staff is specifically trained for the needs of pre-and post-transplant patients. You will get a chest X-ray, EKG, lots of blood work and a urinalysis. You will be instructed to shower with a special medicated soap. Later after surgery you are still given an antibacterial soap to shower; I hate the strong smell of Dial soap and I can smell it on anyone who has showered with it hours earlier. But, I got used to it before I came home. You will be connected to an IV and given antibiotics. I am told all this happened to me, but I have not a single memory of any of it, from the time I arrived at 4 AM until I was wheeled down the hall to the OR eleven hours later at 3 PM. I am unsure whether I have no recollection because of encephalopathy or shock or both. Since I recall the entire drive over to Dallas with Sherri, I suspect I may have been in shock.

It is important to know that many complete the entire preoperative workup and are then told that the transplant is cancelled. This did not happen to me but it had happened to several others I met when I was in the hospital or while living at Twice Blessed House afterwards. Some had been prepped and waited for hours with their hopes high on more than one occasion. Some had gotten as far as being on a gurney in a holding room outside the OR. Emotionally, this can be difficult. There are many reasons that can cause delays to occur. After a donor family has given consent to donate, you will be called if your name comes up as a match on the UNOS computer. You will be on your way to the hospital for all the preoperative testing, even though the donor organ has not been surgically recovered yet. After recovery, the donor organs undergo many tests but the tests can never give the complete status of the organ. The transplant surgeon will examine the organ and be sure it is an acceptable organ, free of lacerations and damage. Fatty livers are unacceptable. Although fatty livers are not life threatening inside a living person, they are not donor friendly. The surgeon will examine the organ at the hospital where your transplant takes place or at the hospital where organ recovery is done. You will not go to the operating room until the donor liver is in the operating room. It should also be noted that what is medically acceptable varies for hospitals. A surgeon may refuse an organ in one hospital but another may use it. Baylor has strict standards of excellence, and because of that strict standard, they have a very good rate of success, thus making them "the" place to get a liver transplant.

Obviously, an organ at less than the normal standard may be used if a patient may die very soon if a liver is not found and an organ becomes available that may be a bridge organ, one that might not be suitable for a lasting transplant but might save a person's life until a medically suitable organ is available.

Paracentesis, fluid removal from my belly and thoracentesis, fluid removal from my lungs, became closer and closer together with some of the paracentesis removing as much as twenty-one liters at once. That sounds like a lot but there are patients who have more than twenty-one liters removed at one time.

On July 13, 2000, I had a transjugular intrahepatic portal-systemic shunt (TIPS) procedure at Baylor. This was to treat portal hypertension, and was done by a radiologist under X-ray guidance. The TIPS procedure reroutes blood flow around the liver and reduces pressure caused by ascites. After a TIPS procedure, the possible complications include: encephalopathy, bleeding into the liver and blockage or narrowing of the shunt. So, when I was dismissed from the hospital, I got right on having one of them—the one thing I feared most, encephalopathy. Already, just from reading about encephalopathy, if I so much as forgot to lock my car door as I usually do, before it locked automatically, I thought I was suffering from encephalopathy. Often with fear comes truth; with the fear of encephalopathy I came to accept the truth, I was sick, very sick and no longer normal, as my ego had demanded. I would have given anything to prove myself wrong.

When I was dismissed on July 16, 2000, I went home with Phyllis and her husband, W.H. I was worried when I did not get better. At this point, I was too sick to care for myself or to know how to care for myself. I was in bed at her house all day except for meals, which I did not want, and when going across the hall to the bathroom. When I awoke on the morning of July 19th Phyllis and I both knew I was not only not better, I was worse. After trying to reach my doctors in Dallas and getting physically worse fast during the day waiting for callbacks that uncharacteristically never came Phyllis took me to the hospital in Paris around 5 PM.

Later, we found out why the doctors in Dallas had not returned the calls. All the telephone lines in her community were not working and there were three emergencies in the community that day. The telephone company reimbursed everyone in the community a month's telephone service.

I recall being wheeled through the emergency entrance of the then St. Joseph's Hospital in a wheel chair, but I do not recall getting inside the ER, only a few feet from the back entrance. In fact, I have no recollection until the next morning other than Dr. Bercher coming toward the room where I was in ER, and he was not wearing his normal white coat he was wearing a suit coat. Much later, when I asked Phyllis about it, she said he had been speaking at a meeting. I had passed out from the accumulation of toxins in my brain. Turns out the TIPS had removed substances necessary to life and had cleansed my body of ammonia, which my diseased liver could not discharge from my blood. With Dr. Bercher on the phone to doctors in Dallas throughout the night he saved me and stabilized me to be transferred one hundred miles away to Baylor Hospital in the morning.

Early in the morning of July 20, 2000, I took an $825, one-hour-and-fifteen-minute ambulance ride to Dallas, Texas and missed the whole thing. Encephalopathy was my complication for the TIPS, and the treatment upon release was more lactulose, the syrupy sweet treat for liver disease patients.

I had lost fifty pounds in the three months since April and continued to lose weight. I was taking diuretics, and still, my weight fluctuated ten or eleven pounds during a single day. I was supposed to drink four cans of Ensure-type supplement per day, but I could not get them down, and what I did get down didn't stay. My constant entertainment was lactulose in with a quick exit and Ensure down with a quick exit. Wal-Mart's Equate brand of Ensure tasted far better and had a less rich taste; so, therefore, it was easier to drink, but it didn't stay down any better. I liked Equate better; much of it wasn't going to stay down anyway and it was cheaper... I didn't have encephalopathy that bad.

It was on my first hospitalization at Baylor that I met Anna Santa Cruz. She was on the 14th floor of Roberts Hospital on the Baylor campus to translate for someone. I saw her in the hall and asked her where something was located. She didn't know but she went to find out then we began talking. I told her about my friends, April and Phyllis, whom she had seen visiting with me earlier. I told Anna that I had been friends with both of them since I was fifteen. I found out that Anna was in the US from El Salvador and how much she missed her family and homeland. She told me about going to visit her homeland and about how she walked miles up a mountain to meet her girlhood friend and her friend walked down the mountain to meet her halfway. She had lost contact with her friend and was hurting because of it. We cried. Anna is a person in touch with her spirit. I enjoyed our talks so much. She was a great comfort in my time of need of great comfort. I was amazed at how a person whom I barely knew could be so in tune with me. She visited me several more times during my stay and on future stays. Even today, we stay in touch by mail.

August 2, 2000, I was dismissed from BUMC and went home with Phyllis again to take more lactulose.

I dared not to tell anyone, but after the TIPS even though I drank lactulose around the clock, I began to experience an increase of encephalopathy. I realize now that Dr. Weinstein knew, and that was the reason for all the added lactulose. At the time the TIPS caused my encephalopathy to worsen, the very nature of the problem prevented me from searching and learning everything there was online to learn about it, as I normally would have done.

Although it was not totally unpleasant, encephalopathy had progressed and I had disassociated states and the feeling I was detached from my body, not real or "outside myself." When I looked out the car window as Phyllis drove home, I was in a detached state but I thought that since I knew it, then it was all right.

On August 3rd, I was bucking to go to my own home. I drove my car the twenty-two miles while in that state of feeling outside myself, still thinking that since I knew how I felt then my driving was all right. I was horrified on the drive going around Loop 286 alone, not sure if I was really all right. With all the fear of encephalopathy I had, a certain amount of fear kept me aware.

At this stage of my illness, no matter how many concessions I made to my disease and illness they were never enough.

Every friend and relative who had email asked the same questions, "How are you?" and "What did the doctor say?" so I started sending a newsletter that I called "Quivered Liver Reports" that contained updates as they happened or when I got home from the hospital after they happened.

After the TIPS failed, my days consisted of many rests and naps, which were unusual because before the July hospitalization I rarely slept at all. My nights and days were the same. I had never been a participant in psychic mind games, but I started to play tapes of waterfalls and rainstorms and practice relaxation techniques, that I had learned years earlier in an attempt to stop migraine headaches. I recommend similar relaxation exercise for anyone awaiting a transplant. Being able to relax on command at the hospital is an advantage. There are meditation exercises that help one to cope with the disease and after the surgery, as does spirituality. Spirituality is not religion. You may have one without the other or you may have both spirituality and religion. Religion is a relationship with God and the rituals and institutions that accompany it. Spirituality is that part of you that is separate from matter; the belief in a Higher Power, force or energy and a feeling of closeness to that Higher Power, force or energy.

I was tormented by intense itching caused by bile salts that build up in the skin of diseased liver patients. I applied Sarno Lotion, with a sponge, several times a day and the itching continued with no interruption as though I had not applied the cooling lotion at all. I ate, or tried to eat, half peanut butter sandwiches, peanut butter toast, cereal and rice pudding because they were easy. I ate bananas and almonds and drank orange juice for potassium when I could eat. I ate, or tried to eat, watermelon, grapes, honeydew, cantaloupe and boiled shrimp in trays I bought already prepared for eating because I could no longer prepare them myself. Blueberries and fruit cups were easy too. I drank as much of the needed Wal-Mart brand of nutritional supplement as I possibly could. I had several nosebleeds everyday, along with foot and leg cramps and charley horses that made me cry and scream and pray and wish that my legs and feet would get numb like a large spot on my left thigh had gotten. Vomiting, or wishing I could, was a regular pastime. I was taking the many medications that resulted in several trips to the bathroom from lactulose and diuretics. I ate spinach from the can and spinach salads trying to increase my potassium. I weighed morning and night to see the difference in fluid weight that was usually ten to twelve pounds in a single day. I measured my girth for ascites with amazing differences in short amounts of time. I had chills, fevers and headaches, something I had not had since the car accident in 1993. My hair quit growing; my hair has since replenished and grows longer and faster with the addition of antirejection drugs after surgery. On my first visit to Dr. Bercher after my transplant surgery he asked about the side effects of my antirejections. I rubbed my forearms and showed him the thicker blond hair there and said, "I'm fuzzy… even my ears." Briefly, he looked a bit puzzled; he thought I meant in the head. Thankfully that fuzziness had gone. My navel herniated from ascites, and I was sure it could be seen underneath my clothes. The doctor told me they would repair it when I got the transplant. They did; I have my inny back.

I spent a lot of time wondering what life would be like after I received a transplant and what it would be like to live without my disease that had been with me so long.

Darlyn voluntarily wallpapered my kitchen for me. Judy came on her lunch break to cut my hair. Bobby came and repaired my garage door. Phyllis came by on her way home from school and checked on me. Beverly and Betty came and took me grocery shopping, which I could barley do, and later they did it for me. Fay brought frozen fruit salads to me that I loved. Sometimes I struggled and drove the five blocks over to Wanda's for lunch or supper because I knew if I stopped making myself go the short distances that I would get so I couldn't go at all. Because she had a cold, Liz left dinner on the doorknob for me, vegetables from the garden. Phyllis got a handicap tag for my car that my ego had kept me from getting sooner. I needed it so badly, but I refused to take up the space of someone who was handicapped. I insisted on being "normal." The handicap car tag was a privilege I did not want to qualify for. Wanda came and stayed the night with me after church on Sunday night. Phyllis Stockton came and stayed with me at a phone call's notice if I needed her. Joann and George came from Dallas to visit me. I talked to my liver buddy, Ruth Ann, more and more often. Several nights Phyllis would come and get me and take me to her house to stay. You can tell by looking at me that I am a good cook, but I rarely had enough energy to cook anymore so Darlyn cooked chicken spaghetti for me, one of the rare foods I could still eat even though not nearly as much as I once had. On August 19th, Fay took me to Dallas to see Dr. Weinstein. I was disoriented and slept all the way. Notes in my journal began to be unreadable. On August 19th, friends began staying with me twenty-four hours a day until my be-normal-or-die ego kicked in again and I insisted I did not need someone twenty-four hours a day everyday. I slept in flannel pajamas with an electric blanket on the bed set on the high setting and on all the time, day and night, because I laid around almost all day. I wore sweats when I was home inside, and when I rarely went outside, even in July and August because I was cold constantly. There was no getting warm. When I returned home from the transplant surgery in mid January I had to remove the electric blanket from my bed and have not had it back on my bed since.

On August 7th, I slept from 2 AM until 5 PM, thirteen hours of totally uninterrupted sleep but also without taking any of the many needed medications. I was disoriented when I awoke and I knew it. I called Phyllis and Dr. Bercher and told them about the many hours sleeping, but not about the disorientation. I was scared about it, and I hoped they would hear, see or know I was disorientated without me telling them. But, I was my ever-calm, informative self, and they didn't catch on. Dr. Bercher instructed me not to stay alone and to catch up on my medications by taking them every two hours. I did as instructed on the medication but I stayed alone, still thinking and believing if I knew I was disoriented that it was all right.

By August 19th, I had lost fifty pounds since April.

Because I was so weak and knew I would get physically worse in the coming months, I dug out smaller clothes and begun to pack the rolling trash barrels that I had bought to pack and take to Dallas. It took days to do small jobs that would have taken me an hour to do before.

On August 28, 2000, I got the letter from my HMO saying they had okayed my transplant. I emailed everyone in my Quivered Liver Report that it was official; my HMO had approved me. I also asked them to put me on their prayer lists and to pray for the family who would suffer great loss in order that I might receive the liver of their deceased loved one. Prayer is not just an answer to our wishes it is to give us a way to cope with the bad times.

I picked up my pager from Texapage who so graciously donates them through LifeGift to those on transplant waiting lists. I thought surely I would wear the thing out, making sure I knew how to work it. I called myself everyday, usually more than once; to be sure it worked correctly. The fact that I was restricted to a distance of about 100 miles from the hospital in Dallas did not matter because I could not go anywhere by myself anyway, not even to Dallas to the doctor or hospital, someone had to drive me. And going a hundred miles, for anything, was not fun; it was a huge chore that I could not accomplish. Just the same, I did not go down the hall in my house without my pager. I thought Baylor would contact me via the pager. I did not know they tried the telephone first and that the beeper was in case I wasn't home. Encephalopathy, I suppose. I was the only person to ever call my pager.

I balanced my bank statement with great difficulty. Numbers were confusing. Encephalopthy was worsening, but I managed.

Barba Covington McCarty

15. Priority: In Order By Importance

Everyone, no matter how humble he may be, has angels to watch over him.
Pope Pius XII

On August 28th, Alyssa Plette, my pre-transplant coordinator and the person who kept me sane, well almost, while I waited for a transplant called and told me because of my worsened condition I had been put on the 2B list—not hospitalized, but a higher status than other non-hospitalized candidates waiting for a liver. She called it 2B, priority status. As waits go in the transplant world, Alyssa had no idea how long for me to expect the wait to be. Because I was B-positive blood type, there wasn't even an average waiting time.

In late August and early September, I became devastatingly ill. My TIPS became clogged and quit working, so I was huge with ascites. According to Dr. Weinstein, the risk was too great to chance removing the TIPS and inserting another one, since I had gotten so ill after it was installed in July. At my visit with him on September 7th, he informed me that he was going to take my case before the board and try to get me moved up on the list again; I had just been moved up a week earlier.

Priority. In order by importance. Dying was not an option for me. But, without a transplant, it was now certain. When a person gets to priority status for a transplant, that person is not *possibly* going to die, not *maybe* going to die, not *probably* going to die, that person *is* going to die without a transplant. I *was* going to die and my expiration date was extremely close.

After the shunt failed, I had to turn up the positive thoughts. I was too weak to hold a book to read, even in bed, so I played self-help tapes and the comedy and encouraging tapes of Liz Curtis Higgs. Thank you Lizzie for the encouragement. This book came about as a result of my writing a letter to Liz Curtis Higgs thanking her for encouraging words and the laughter she provided me on the tapes I played during my illness. That letter that I never mailed to her, turned in to this book. I played audio books by Lewis Grizzard over and over again. Thank you Lewis for the laughter. I played Leo Buscaglia's *Loving Each Other* and *Born for Love, Fried Green Tomatoes at the Whistle Stop Café,* and anything by Tom Bodett, even his *End of the Road,* which I was afraid might be about death and dying when I first saw it, but it wasn't. I practiced relaxation techniques that I had learned years before and had taught my niece, Destiny, who has migraines.

During this time, I shut down emotionally. I no longer kept my grateful journal; I made entries in the area of medical matters only. One day, amongst my medical entries I wrote, "I am just thankful." The alternate routes of travel I had devised to take to save energy and time were no longer needed. If I got to the car and discovered I left my handbag, coat or keys inside, I just didn't do the chore I had set out to do; the added energy used to return and get a left item was the energy I had saved to do the chore, and there was no excess to handle problems no matter how small. I no longer cried, even when I tried to do the simple tasks I couldn't finish. I was whipped, so, I just didn't attempt to do the tasks anymore. My laugh was a forced smile often misunderstood as no interest. I had no energy even to get angry. Excitement, even fear was non-existent; there was not a place for either of those emotions. Even walking on grass or gravel was too much because there is so much more energy required than to walk on straight concrete walkways. I no longer wanted to go anywhere, even if someone picked me up and drove me, because the extra effort required to get in and out of a vehicle that was higher or lower than what I could do with ease. Everyone I know has an SUV or pickup truck of some sort. I did not sit in my recliner because removing the leaned-back adjustment was too much for the energy and strength I had. I no longer kept time with my fingers tapping on the steering wheel to music on the car radio; I no longer played the car radio. I just didn't have the energy for it. I did not experience wonder like I once did at the size of a baby's hand. In the years of illness, I lost the tender me that used to be. I lost the desire to go for a drive to look at spring flowers or autumn colors. I am thankful the tender me has returned with a passion of a new lover. Once again the seasons make me think of God. I am at an Eldorado, where I am rich in the opportunity of life. I cannot get enough of the wonder of winter's snow, spring's flowers, summer's blue lakes and autumn's leaves and a baby's hands. And, yes, that's me jiving down the road, tapping my steering wheel to the sounds of a pop-music station on the radio. I have curls back in my hair, because I felt like a trip to the beauty shop and could stay up long enough to get a perm. Before I had to have the easiest do-nothing hairdo I could get—a wash-and-dry-in-less-than-two-minutes style. The art of smiling has returned. I am back, and I have an ever-growing appreciation for living.

Those relaxation techniques were just another little bit of heaven after I had the transplant as I played Baylor's relaxation channel 18 and relaxed while Beverly and Betty drowned themselves, and anyone else around them, in pools of un-relaxation and worry. I had a platform of faith that I would get a liver and that I would get it soon enough, though I still thought the time was far away.

I had told my cousins, who were worried about my beginning to look emaciated at Covington Cousin's Day, my family reunion, at the end of April, that I would have to get a lot worse physically to get on the transplant list. I thought I had to get one rung before death on the ladder of living. I had arrived, even by my own standards. Just three months after the reunion, in

August, I was fifty pounds lighter and had turned visibly yellow, my least favorite color.

Early in September, I found out how bad the encephalopathy was. I was overdrawn at my bank by $400.90. My checkbook showed that I had over $300 in the account. My mind was boggled. Literally. I could not figure out what I had done and could not even refigure the book. I'm not good with numbers at my best mindset, but you should see me dealing with numbers while under the misdirection of encephalopathy. Not only could I not figure out what I had done, I could not get dressed and go to the bank and take care of the problem because I was beyond going anywhere then. Bobby called me that night and when I answered the phone crying and told him why he went to the bank the next morning and deposited into my account the amount I was overdrawn without my asking him. After I returned home from having the transplant, almost a year later, I found a note in my bill book that I had written concerning the $400.90 that he deposited into my account. With him protesting loudly, I paid him back.

After a weight loss of fifty pounds in only weeks, my weight suddenly increased by twenty-five pounds. My ankles, legs, face, everything was swollen without the TIPS shunt working. I continued to swell and could hardly breath from the fluid buildup. I slept, when I rarely did sleep, sitting almost straight up, with my head raised on the two wedge pillows I had used when my neck was broken, then I stacked two more pillows atop the two wedges.

At the September 13th appointment with Dr. Weinstein for a paracentesis to remove fluid from my belly, I had written on my question sheet to ask him if I was going to make it until I got a liver, but I didn't ask him. Although I had never asked the question of him before, I was afraid of his answer, which I feared would be, "We sure hope so." I severely needed a "Yes."

My September 13th Quivered Liver Report read as follows: "Today was not good. I had 20½ pounds of fluid in the ten days since I was last there. Dr. Weinstein couldn't get to it; he said it was too high on the abdomen near the liver and couldn't be reached without danger of injury elsewhere. He sent me to X-ray for a sonoguided paracentesis where they can see where the fluid is to remove it. I am puffed up like a bullfrog, swollen everywhere. Only 5½ pounds of the fluid could be tapped off today. It was the least productive trip I have had to make. Maybe sometimes I can send y'all some good news. In the meantime this is it. Thanks for your concern and prayers. Love, Barb."

Quivered Liver Report, September 20th: "I am just up for awhile and thought I'd send an update. I had to call the doctor in Dallas today; I had so much fluid and pressure. The doctor in Dallas called X-ray department here and set me up for an immediate sonoguided paracentesis. The pressure on my ribcage, breastbone and left side is somewhat better, but I still fell like a bum. Dr. said that most likely that's how I'll feel until I get a liver. I keep that baby boy on my mind that Destiny and Kurt are about to have in late January or early February. I can't wait to see him. I am expecting any day for one of you to put me on your "block sender" list. Love, Barb"

In the September 29th Quivered Liver Report emailed at 12:00 AM to my friends and family, I wrote: I got back from Dallas today about 5 PM and am just now "sort of" rested, thus this midnight email. Dr. Weinstein thinks that I need to leave the fluid on the liver area until it gets extremely painful or uncomfortable since the risk of fluid staying on is less than the removal via an invasive procedure to remove it every five or six days that might cause bleeding or infection. And, so it is. I may burst in the meantime, but maybe it will no longer hurt after I do! Ha. My navel is ruptured from the bulge of ascites. He said just keep an eye on it and be sure it doesn't get enflamed or strangulated (whatever that is! Ha.) Doesn't sound good though. As soon as I feel better, about tomorrow or Saturday, I will be checking that word strangulated out in the literature around here. They say the waiting list for 2B (priority) patients is usually six to nine months, and I have in two and half so, as George Jefferson used to say, "I'm movin' on up." My forever friend, Joann Smith Graber, has been here since Tuesday and took me to Dallas today to the doctor. She's been a Godsend. Aren't friends wonderful? That's the quivered liver report. Thanks for caring. Barb."

I continued to expand my girth and gain weight and have a fever. Having an elevated temperature worried me greatly even though it was a low-grade fever staying about 100 degrees. If you are sick or have a temperature, you cannot get a transplant even if a liver becomes available for you. I had a temperature on October 1, 2000, and no more that week. The fever suddenly stopped, after weeks of having slightly elevated temperatures.

Even though I had been moved up on the list, I still had no doubt my transplant was a long way off.

Many die while waiting "in order of importance" on the priority list.

16. More Family Matters

Blessed is he whose transgression is forgiven...
Psalms 32:1

I am a very independent person, and, before my illness got so severe and stripped away everything private, I was a very private person. I am not one who asks anyone anything concerning monetary matters, and I am not one to divulge my own.

My sisters finally fully acknowledged my illness, and imminent death, when I experienced the TIPS shunt complications in July. They became increasingly interested in my finances and how things would be handled when I died, which is what they thought, without a doubt, was about to happen. They had me dressed in pink and ready to lay out in a pink (I'm sure) casket which wasn't going to happen if I did die, but they didn't know it, because they weren't open to my discussing the matters of my body being donated "to science" which I had already done paperwork for, without their knowledge. I thought I would be a great study in long-term HCV in a classroom of would-be doctors at UT Southwest Medical School.

It was the classic "Barb's dying; who's got the will" scene, not of greed but of necessity, to handle an emergency situation they had not prepared for but I had. Up until I got so very ill after the shunt failed in July, it had been like my illness was a family secret not to be discussed, and if by not discussing it, possibly it would go away. It was during this time after some family incidents occurred, that I wrote a letter and sent a copy to all of my siblings explaining that I had executed a Physicians Directive. Being the private person that I am, I explained to them how the Physicians Directive worked but not how I had directed the physician. I told them I had prepared a Power of Attorney, a Durable General Power of Attorney and a Guardianship Designation should the need arise and whom I had designated as such. There was dissention because I chose a close friend to act on my behalf and not a relative. However, I had to have someone who was in Paris to handle my life, because my life was in Paris. I had to have someone that was familiar with my life. My sisters' denial of my illness had made them not familiar with my life. I told them I had a will and that it was in a safe place if I died, "which I won't," I said. In the letter I made statements like "should I die prematurely, and I won't" and "should I die sooner than expected, and I won't" and "I am not in need of a funeral service yet, and I won't be," and "I have left instructions for a memorial service if needed, but they won't be needed."

Yes, I was scared, sad, hurt and very, very ill when I wrote the letter. I was far too sick to be dealing with everyday life that was speedily escaping me, let alone petty fuses over who I had chosen to run my life. My letter conveyed my intentions in the way that I have of getting my point across. I also wrote: "I am going to be temporarily "on hold" while I receive a lifesaving transplant, so, let's not forget I will be back in good form and will, indeed, know who did what during my absence. I hope you will make your actions worthwhile and can live with them afterwards. Make it so you have no regrets when I look into your face once again, and I will. A transplant is a lifesaving procedure to better a life that might otherwise be shortened by the disease that I have, HCV. With the medical giant steps forward, I do expect my liver transplant to be just that, a lifesaving procedure for me. I will be back."

I was determined to live. At the point I wrote the letter, I am still unaware if I was trying to convince my sisters I was going to live or myself. I thought I was convinced I was going to live, but I had prepared as if I wasn't, which is my way. I would make a good Boy Scout. I am prepared.

17. Brain Death

I n the past, *death* was considered to be a basic term used to describe the cessation of life. Death occurred when both respiratory and circulatory functions stopped. With the development of medical equipment like ventilators, that keep the patient breathing though he cannot breathe on his own, the term *death* has been reexamined and redefined.

Now, two terms describe death—brain death and cardiac death. Both terms unequivocally mean death. They are used only to differentiate the means of death.

Brain death is not the same as a coma. Brain activity is still present when a patient is in a coma; therefore, there is a chance the patient may regain consciousness. A brain-dead patient is declared dead by neurological criteria. The patient is permanently unable to think, see, hear or feel. Brain death occurs when a person has suffered a severe head injury, such as trauma, brain hemorrhage or stroke, or any prolonged deficiency of oxygen to the brain.

There is a critical organ shortage. According to the United Network for Organ Sharing (UNOS), in the year 2000, when I was transplanted, there were 5,984 cadaveric organ donors. There were 22,854 lifesaving organ transplants. Even with 22,854 transplants there were still 79,346 registrations on waiting lists at the end of the year and 5,800 died in the year 2000 while waiting. The numbers are staggering.

You, or a loved one, is fourteen times as likely to become ill and be placed on a transplant waiting list—waiting for a life-saving organ that may not come—than you are to experience death by brain death. And, when you, or your loved one, get on that transplant waiting list you are very likely to die waiting for a donated organ to save your life because there are not enough donors.

While liver transplants are not the answer to eliminating liver disease, transplants are the only hope for survival many liver patients have. But there just are not enough organ donors to meet the demand. The same applies to other's waiting and in need for organs other than livers; those waiting for hearts, kidneys, lungs, pancreas and intestines face the same fate.

Barba Covington McCarty

18. Autumn, My Favorite Season

Suddenly an angel of the Lord appeared...
Acts 12:7

I filled out the papers for disability, something else my ego would not allow me to do even though the doctors had advised it. I was afraid if I admitted that I was disabled I would become disabled. The fact that I was, and had been for at least nine years already, did not affect my thoughts that I wasn't unless it was declared on paper.

I never told anyone, but all through the month of September I had thoughts concerning my impending death. I had serenity about it. If I died, it was my time, and it was all right. Now, my life itself was in my file of "Things I Have No Control Over." If I got a transplant I was supposed to; if I did not get one, then I was not supposed to. I did not resign to die, but I resigned to the fact that I might, and I was not scared. Death is no longer the fear it once was.

Even with all these thoughts going on inside me, when someone asked, "How are you?" I still replied, "I'm just great." If it was someone very close to me, I usually said, "I'm just great, can you tell?" It lightened the moment.

In early September, I began updating paperwork. I did paperwork for living, I wrote volumes of instructions to Phyllis whom I had designated as my Power of Attorney so she could run my life while I was away. I updated my Living Will, the Medical Power of Attorney and Medical Directives, all that stuff we normally ignore when we are admitted to a hospital.

Then I did the paperwork that would be necessary if I was incapacitated after surgery; I designated a guardian if the need arose. I wrote letters, addressed and stamped them, to be mailed when I was hospitalized to temporarily turn off my cell phone, Internet service and TV cable and let my lawn service know someone else would be paying my bill while I was away.

And, yes, I did the paperwork to die. I updated my will, wrote instructions to my family and letters to people I love.

When I got home I had a paper shredding party all by myself. I sent in the paperwork to donate my body to UT Southwest Medical School. I thought if I died before I got a transplant that I would be a great study for the effects of long-term hepatitis C to a classroom of would-be doctors. I am glad that is one field trip I missed.

On September 11, 2000, at two in the afternoon, I took all the updated paperwork to my bank box. I was exhausted and felt so bad that I sat in my car and cried before I went into the bank and again before I got out of the car at home after I finished the task.

Phyllis was ill and had been for a month or so. She had been diagnosed with Respiratory Syncytial Virus, RSV. RSV is contagious, so I couldn't be around her.

* * *

During the last days of September 2000, about two hours away from where I live, a nurse and her husband, married for nearly six years, took an autumn stroll through his family cemetery. As they stood looking over the headstones, the husband said that if anything ever happened to him, he wanted to be buried there. He also said that he wanted to be an organ donor. The wife listened to her husband's wishes, hoping that she would never have to comply with them.

A few days after the cemetery visit, on October 3rd, that man had what seemed to be a minor accident. While he was working on the hydraulics of his SUV door, the door fell and hit him on the head. It hurt like a bump on the head does, but the pain was not severe enough for him to see a doctor.

* * *

Even though it was at least a year early, during the first week of October, I was finishing packing the rolling trash barrels with items I needed to live in Dallas and slowly loading into the trunk of my car all the items that I would need while I was hospitalized and making endless lists for Phyllis and me.

* * *

The first week of October was quite different for the wife and family of the man who had sustained the bump on the head by his SUV door. Three days later, he passed out and was taken to a local hospital by ambulance.

* * *

By then my journal had become a medical record. Nosebleeds, throw ups and bowel movements are mostly not listed for the obvious reason that I was too busy right then to write them down. Neither are the medications lactulose and potassium because they were on the counter for the day, and I knew I had managed them all when I finished them. Because I was in bed did not mean I was asleep.

On Wednesday, October 4, I wrote:

"4 AM, I woke up; Cheerios and milk; 9 AM, got up; 9:30 AM, meds, Edecrin, Prevacid; I felt so bad today I did not do all the medicals in my journal today, but I took all the meds on time. Took until 9 PM to feel anyway like getting up at all. Hernia is more distended. Back to bed."

And, on October 4th I also got out the lists I had prepared for Phyllis and myself and updated them once again.

The plan was that no matter when I got the call, Phyllis would take me to Dallas for the transplant; she would be my designated driver to go get my new working liver. But, Phyllis was sick with RSV, a virus that spreads easily from person to person through contact with respiratory secretions. She was better, but we feared her virus was still contagious and were waiting for her next appointment with her doctor to find out.

On Thursday, October 5, I went to the only place I went on those days, Dr. Bercher's office and the lab there. He was out of the office so I saw Susan Scholtz, CFNP, the nurse practitioner whom I was very comfortable with; she had worked previously in a liver-transplant setting.

I was suffering from hypokalemia, a potassium level below 3.5. Potassium is one of the body's major ions. The symptoms of hypokalemia are many, mine were weakness, nausea and vomiting, leg cramps, lowered blood pressure, lethargy and decreased muscle strength. Diuretics (aka water pills) frequently are the cause of hypokalemia, and I was on massive doses of diuretics due to ascites, fluid on my belly. My potassium tablets were K-Dur, a chalky, white tablet that is 7/8 of an inch in length and 3/8 of an inch wide. I tried to get six of those watermelon size pills down four times a day (a total of 24 per day) when, at that time in my disease, getting water alone to stay down was a major feat. It is hard to explain to someone who hasn't done it; but if you can't eat or drink, then you can't. It has nothing to do with taste or "making yourself." Taking potassium was an all day process; I gagged as I tried to take the pills, and I threw the pills back up repeatedly. Once I decided that if I could dry-swallow them then I could keep them down. Not so. I choked on them. One choking on one half of a KDur cured that ill-devised plan. Most days I got them all down but I was unable to keep them down. So, I cut them in half and set them out in my bathroom, because that is where you throw up, in a blue ¼ cup-measuring cup. A days worth of half-pills filled it to the rim. After I got past the gagging, I took one half then another half, and then I waited. If I didn't throw those two halves back up then I'd take another two halves. If I did throw up, or if they disintegrated in the gagging process, I added two more halves to the pile of K-Dur. I feared causing a bleed by vomiting since my portal hypertension had worsened. I had several nosebleeds a day, and if a nosebleed happened when I was vomiting or shortly afterwards, I was horrified that it was a gastroenterological bleed. When I returned home three-and-a-half months after my transplant surgery, the first thing I did after using my very own potty was flush the ½ tablets of K-Dur that were still sitting on my sink. I hope I never have to take another K-Dur.

Susan instructed the lab to draw blood and gave me the number to get her directly so I could call her if I needed anything during the night or later. I made an appointment to go back to her office again on Friday, the next day, to get labs checked after taking yet another increased amount of potassium.

Sherri, who is married to my cousin, Ira, came and picked me up on Thursday evening, and we went to eat. When she was leaving, with her car already rolling backwards out of the driveway, she commented, through a small opening of the window (because of the rain) about my getting a call for a liver. She frequently did this. Normally, I treated those comments from her, and everyone else, with little fanfare, mostly because I didn't feel well, but also, to keep from getting myself in the waiting-for-the-call mode. I had at least a year more to wait. On this night I replied, "I can't get a call; Phyllis is still sick." Sherri rolled her car window farther down, ignoring the rain that fell on her arm and face, and pulled her car closer to the garage where I was standing out of the rain and said, "If you get the call, I'll take you." I forced a smile and said nothing. I knew it was far too early for the call. Sherri continued with, "I'm serious. I'll take you." I knew she was serious. I also knew I was not going to get the call.

Phyllis was much better and had an appointment with her doctor on Friday, the next day, to get the RSV checked and to be sure she was no longer contagious. We were not taking any chances on my catching the virus, so I talked to her frequently but still had not seen her in a month or so.

After Sherri left, I went in the house and rested but didn't sleep. Later I got up and got on the computer and answered email and read the jokes that I had received, which were many back then from friends keeping in touch and trying to add some fun to my life. When I couldn't sleep I spent time on my computer, researching anything about liver transplant.

In my journal on Thursday, October 5, I wrote: "178 lbs.; 54 (girth); 12:45 AM, I went to sleep but was already in bed; 3:30 AM, almost three hours sleep! Great; ½ and ½ Equate and milk, 6 oz.; Meds; 3:45 AM, back to bed; 10 AM, still no sleep, Got up. Hernia is more distended. ½ and ½ Equate and milk, ¼ C. beans and rice (that Sherri and Ira had brought me) and ½ piece of cornbread and a medium raw potato; 12:20 PM, Meds, Prevacid; 4 PM, after doctor visit I drove to Long John Silver's for fish, something new, ½ piece of fish, yuk! 2 crab pieces, Yuk! Bite of coleslaw, Yuk! Ended up eating a red raw potato and 2 hushpuppies; Meds, potassium, Atarax, Neomycin, Edecrin, lactulose; 4:20 PM, to bed; Went with Sherri to eat, then couldn't; 8:15 PM, ½ small apple, 6 grapes, salt-free potato chips and iced tea; 8:45 PM, meds, potassium, Neomycin; 10:30 PM, back to bed, rest, still cannot sleep; Susan Scholtz prescribed more potassium today, and I am to go to the lab tomorrow at 2 PM to check it again. It was very low. Another 'feel bad all day' day."

* * *

The wife and family of the man in the hospital declared brain dead by a hit on the head by his SUV door prayed their loved one would live and got second opinions in hopes of it. When the worst was the answer, amidst their pain and loss, they discussed the matter of donating his organs. Later that day the nurse complied with the wishes of her husband; she arranged for donations of his organs. Her prayer request was an instance where God said no. I had no idea of any of the events in that man's and his family's life then; I learned of the events later... but God's no to them became my yes.

* * *

On Friday, October 6, I wrote: "12:00 AM, ½ and ½ Equate and milk; 12:15 AM, to bed; 12:45 AM, My tummy hurts, is very large with ascites. I can't sleep or lay."

The 12:45 AM entry was the last one for Friday morning, October 6, 2000. I went to the living room and sat in the recliner in the dark until 1:20 AM when I decided to try another time to get comfortable enough to lay in bed.

I stopped by the bathroom, drank some water and took two halves of a K-Dur that I managed to keep down, then walked to my bed. Just as I sat down on my bed, the phone rang.

You know how when the phone rings late at night or in the early hours of the morning you instantly think, "What's wrong?" That was my second thought. My first thought was that it was too late, even for Bobby to call me, as he sometimes did after he got home when he got off work at eleven. I answered to a woman who said, "Mrs. McCarty." "Yes," I replied. "This is Kathy at Baylor Hospital. We have a liver for you." I breathed in and could not exhale. There was a long silence on the line. Kathy said, "Mrs. McCarty." Another silence.

Finally, I said, "Are you sure?" Kathy said she was sure. She asked me if I was sick or had a temperature. I said I wasn't and asked her again if she was sure. I could not believe there was a liver for me so soon. She said the surgery would be at 3 PM that afternoon, almost fourteen hours away. I asked her once again if she was sure; she told me again that she was and asked me how long it would take me to get there. I told her I lived in Paris and it would take only two hours or so.

She said, "Okay, we'll see you about four then."

I said, "Oh, you want me to come now." Yes, she did. "Why am I coming now if it's not until three tomorrow?" 3 PM tomorrow was actually today but it was nighttime, and I hadn't even been to bed yet, not that I could have slept after Kathy's call.

She said, "We have lots of things to do to you beforehand."

I said, "I can't believe I have one; are you sure?" Kathy must have thought I hadn't taken my lactulose because she asked me if there was anyone there with me. When I said there wasn't, she told me to get a pencil and write down the directions of where to go when I got to the hospital. It was a good thing she did.

When I hung up the phone I was sure of but one thing; Kathy was sure. I sat on the bed crying a few short minutes then dried it up to make the necessary calls. I dialed Sherri's number, and she answered with a sleepy, "Hello."

I said, "I've been called." She immediately woke up and without a sign in her voice of having been asleep she said, "I'll be right there," as though she had been given a code word to jump into action, and hung up the phone.

I hung up and called Phyllis, "I've been called," I said again. I told her I had called Sherri and that she was on her way to take me. We cried. I told her the surgery was scheduled for 3 PM on Friday afternoon. She said something about seeing me later, after she went to the doctor.

I got out the list I had prepared of the last minute things to do when I got the call. I turned off the telephones and the answering machine, put a lamp on a timer, put the thermostat at 55 degrees, disconnected my computer and TV, cleaned any smellies out of the refrigerator (which were few in those days), took the trash out, etc. All the while, I debated whether to call my little sister, Beverly, then or wait until she would be awake to call her. She and I had fussed on the phone earlier before her bedtime, so I decided that if the shoes were reversed, I would not want her to wait to call me. I rang her number and when she answered I said, "I've been called."

Phyllis and I called back and forth a few times with matters I do not remember, mostly excitement, I think.

In less than twenty-minutes, Sherri had gotten dressed, packed a bag and driven the seven miles or so to my house. I was standing beside the passenger-side door putting my Daytimer organizer that Sherri gave me in the car when she rolled into the driveway and bounded out of her car in the rain and ran over to the driver's side of my car and flung her bag in the back floorboard. She ran back to her car and got her purse, locked her car and ran back to my car where I was standing waiting for her to slow the pace. She didn't. I said, "Sherri, you're going to have to slow down, you're going to get me in a tizzy." I was my ever in-control self where no tizzies were allowed, especially in recent years when there was no energy for a tizzy.

Phyllis and I had already talked about the fact that I might get to Dallas then not get a transplant, but Sherri and I hadn't. On the drive over to Dallas in the rain, I told Sherri that I might not get a liver, even after the drive over, lots of things could happen, and it might not work out. Sherri is positive about everything, all the time. She said, "It'll work out." I felt as sure as she did, but it was a possibility.

Although none of these emotions showed, I felt like I had won an emotional lottery; I was anxious but not excited, scared but not full of fear, hopeful but not expectant. With end-stage liver disease, a person's visible emotions are near non-existent because emotions take energy and I had none.

As we drove, I told Sherri to slow down, we were not in a hurry. It was raining and there was a light fog in places. I said, "Slow down; I have come too far to get this liver to take a chance on not getting it because we wrecked on the way to the hospital." She would slow down then almost immediately speed up again. After several reminders to slow down near the town of Commerce, forty-seven miles down the road and almost half way to Baylor she finally slowed down. I wanted to stop at the Knox station on the Interstate for a break, but Sherri didn't think we should. It wasn't a choice for me; I was taking diuretics and lactulose, so we stopped. I didn't eat or drink anything because I had had surgery before, and I knew that was a no no, and didn't want anything either. Sherri kept saying she couldn't believe I was so calm. I expected to feel exhilarated… and I did; she just couldn't tell because I had no energy to outwardly show it. In my mind, I had dress rehearsed this run for several years, even before I had the pre-transplant evaluation and was put on the waiting list.

When we got to the front door of Roberts Hospital on the Baylor campus, Sherri let me out and unloaded the bag I had packed for the first day's stay at the hospital, my Daytimer, my handbag and hers. Two men who were cleaning in the lobby let me in and brought the bags inside for me. I sat on a bench inside the door near the gift shop and waited while Sherri parked the car. I was exhausted and welcomed the wait so I could rest. Baylor is a huge campus, and it took her awhile to park the car and walk back up to the entrance in the rain. When she got there, I had the note out with the instructions of where to go that Kathy had given me over the phone. I handed it to Sherri, and she asked the two men which way to go. One began giving directions to us and then decided to guide us there. Since 14 Roberts was being remodeled, the place to report to was different than the usual place to report for liver transplant. Sherri and the nice man who was guiding us carried my bag, my Daytimer organizer and my handbag along with Sherri's things. It was quite a walk that I didn't think I could make even though I carried nothing. Just as I said I could not go any further, we were there, I suppose. I don't know where "there" was, and I do not remember getting there, checking in, going to the room or putting on a gown.

Friday seems mostly like a blur to me now. I do remember there were several of those very official looking papers; the "get ready, you may die" documents of which I would sign many more before I was dismissed from the hospital. By the time I signed all of them I thought they could kill me and take my body directly to the basement and what I envisioned as the dark catacombs of the hospital. I also envisioned the research lab that I had donated myself to if I didn't make it through the surgery and a full classroom of would-be transplant surgeons were also there.

I do remember calling Susan Scholtz's desk number that she had given me the day before. I got Dorese Basinger, who was Susan's assistant, and told her I wouldn't be in at two that day that I was in Dallas and I had a liver transplant scheduled for 3 PM. Her voice broke as she said, "I'm glad. Not that you won't be in, but that you're getting a liver."

When I received the call from Kathy at 1:20 AM, I had been without sleep for twenty-two hours, since 3:30 AM on Thursday morning, and I had slept only three hours then. It would be fourteen more hours before I was put to sleep in the OR. I was without sleep for thirty-six hours but I couldn't tell it; I certainly wasn't sleepy.

I do recall the ride to the long awaited and desired location—OR. The ride on a rolling bed down the long halls of a hospital must be akin to a luge ride at the Winter Olympics. I was icy cold and shivering, without the benefit of winter clothing that athletes wear in the Olympics, in my thin backless hospital gown with a sheet for covering on an out-of-control-fast bed, without the protection given to a luge, controlled by someone else, in my case, Patrick, the hospital's official luge operator. Patrick and I would make that ride down the halls on the hospital luge many more times in the next few weeks.

19. Surgery

I, Jesus, have sent my angel...
Revelations 22:16

I have few recollections of the OR before I was out. I was cold, bone cold and visibly shivering like an Eskimo outside the igloo without a fur.

There were several nurses working like they were running an ant farm each knowing their job and doing it like machines. I was moved from Patrick's luge onto the standard operating room platform, that resembles an ironing board with no place for your arms. My backless gown was removed from me and now I was cold like a naked Eskimo outside the igloo.

I lay flat on my back naked, but covered with a sheet, as a nurse began apologizing for what she was about to do to me by saying, "I know you are cold; it's cold in here and this is going to be really cold. I have to pour this all over you. I'm sorry, but it is something that must be done before surgery." I am sure the liquid contained antibiotics or antiseptics that made sure I was germ free. She was right the liquid was really cold. Any germ that dared jump on me now would freeze, lest my shaking like a dog shakes water sent them running. The next memory I have is hearing talk about several more warm blankets as I continued to shiver underneath the ones already there.

My last memory before I asked to be "put out" was of a young man—whom I now believe was Dr. Sanchez, not yet on staff when I received my transplant—with dark hair leaning over a large, shiny, silver mixing bowl like I make oatmeal cookies in at home. He reached a gloved hand inside the bowl and carefully touched whatever was in the bowl. I knew that was my donor's liver. I was terrified that he was going to show it to me. I did not want to see the liver—not even the liver that was going to save my life.

Like I do before every surgery I have ever had, I asked why I knew all that was happening and laughingly told them I was chicken; I wanted to be asleep. They said it would be only a few more minutes. I looked over at the character still peering into the silver bowl, touching what I knew was my donor's liver. He was the last thing I saw.

I was in surgery nine-and-a-half hours. I used seventeen units of blood. I was astounded by the number but was told that was an unusually small number of units for a liver transplant. Liver transplants vary in length from five to eighteen hours. The reasons for surgery taking longer are; if a bypass must be performed to maintain kidney function and blood flow to the lower extremities and if the old liver is hard to remove. There were no problems. Later when I asked Dr. Molmenti why it took nine-and-a-half hours instead of five he said the extra time was needed for extracting my old liver.

April, Phyllis and Sherri waited in the surgery waiting room until Dr. Molmenti came out on Saturday morning at 12:30 AM to inform them that the surgery was over. Beverly and Betty had gone to Baylor Plaza Hotel and went to sleep; sleep is their escape.

I do not recall it but they tell me I was connected to a respirator, which is connected to a tube that was placed in my windpipe to help me breathe. There was a nasogastric tube (NG), a small plastic tube inserted during surgery in my nose that passed to my stomach to keep my stomach empty of residual food that I had before surgery and to remove the juices that are normally produced. Liquid nutrition came through a feeding tube, and I had a catheter to monitor my kidney function. From the Mercedes incision were three grenade-like bulbs for draining any excess blood or fluid that is common after a transplant. I did not have a T-tube immediately but had one later after a second surgery that remained in place, aggravating me for weeks. There were several IV lines to give fluids and medications that were capped off by HEP-LOK and used only when medications were given. There was a Triple Lumen Catheter in my jugular vein on the right side of my neck with three ports used to draw blood, administer medications and for parenteral nutrition if needed. I could not see the thing—that felt like three AAA batteries cut in half, glued together side by side and nailed to my neck—and was too out of it to question why it got so much attention. The Triple Lumen Catheter is wonderful even if it does become a bit aggravating just by being there; many, many, many sticks by drawing blood and giving medications are avoided with it in place. After it was removed, I looked like I had been the victim of a one-handed strangler's attack.

I have three recollections of my time in ICU. First, I was hot. Hot for the first time in at least twelve years. I awakened, throwing the cover off me and raising the tail of my gown and fanning with it. Of course, there was nothing underneath as I had a catheter in place. The nurse told me repeatedly to keep my gown down. I kept doing the fanning bit over and over until the nurse got irritated with me. She kept telling me, "Mrs. McCarty, there are men in here." I kept telling her to "Get 'em out." I knew I was doing it, but I didn't care. I did not understand why there were men in there, because I was laying on my back and could not see them. The fact that I had no idea where I was did not matter to me; what mattered was I was hot.

In my stay at Baylor, she is the only nurse who got anything near hateful with me. I was angry with her for a while, but one needs to keep the air as clear as possible so when I was put in ICU later and could not pick her out, I figured I might not have remembered it all or accurately. But, from that second trip to ICU when I do remember everything, I also don't know why she didn't just pull the curtain around my bed and let me fan with my gown tail!

My first memory, other than feeling like I might be in hell, was Phyllis standing far across the room with her arms crossed and looking at me; for some reason I thought she looked like a paper doll across the room, and when she saw I was awake, she waved to me. Later when I told her that was my first memory when I woke up, she said the nurses let them come in but that they had to stand far away and just look at me because I was irritated. I was. I was hot! Until I brought that memory up to Phyllis almost a year later, I had thought that it really didn't happen, that I just thought I had seen her as a paper doll standing across the room waving to me.

My third memory was on Saturday afternoon when my niece, Destiny, and her husband Kurt came to visit me. Destiny was five months pregnant. I hadn't seen her since her pregnancy started showing, and I wanted to see how big she was. She tucked her hands under her tummy and turned sideways. I insisted she raise her blouse so I could see her belly. She did it. That was my first glimpse of my coming great-nephew, Kameron, although it was a glimpse "in the round."

Many say they have a terrible experience with being extubated when they removed the ventilator. My recollection of it could be classified as almost not at all.

After I was told I was going to go to a room, a male nurse disconnected the arterial line that was put in my left wrist for monitoring blood pressure and drawing blood. Suddenly, when my arm was laying across my stomach, I felt wetness. My wrist was bleeding profusely; the nurse applied pressure to stop the bleeding but I kept bleeding. The hospital gown I was wearing and the bed sheet became red and sticky. The nurse kept applying pressure and I kept bleeding underneath his hand. I was still a bit stupid, as we are after liver transplant surgery, but after a while even in my state of not being quite there, I became worried and so did the nurse. He called for another nurse to apply the pressure while he called my doctor. About the time he reached the doctor by phone, the bleeding stopped. I had to have a complete bed change and bath before leaving ICU and going to the room. I am sure the nurse had to have a bath also, since he looked like he had committed an axe murder.

Some say they do have pain, but the good thing for me was that there was not much site pain. In research, I had read that there wouldn't be much pain due to the severance of nerves and the use of steroid medications.

The average stay in ICU depends on a patient's body's tolerance of the surgical procedure as well as the preoperative medical condition. I don't know which day I got out of ICU.

While hospitalized, twice daily I had the pleasure of the company of the transplant team of doctors along with post-transplant coordinators, social workers, dieticians and doctors-in-training. The room was full and swollen out into the hall when the transplant team, most with their clipboards, entered my room for rounds.

After I am put to sleep for surgeries I do not want to wake up. After transplant was no exception. Dr. Levy would enter the room with all his ducklings following behind him and I would talk to him with my eyes closed. He would mention it and I'd open them for a quick peek then close them again until he insisted I keep my eyes open. He didn't understand that and neither do I. I just do it.

Lots of prayers were said for me. I had spiritual support from people I had never heard of. For a while, I hogged the prayer lists of every church where I knew anyone who knew anyone who attended there. My sisters called me everyday that they weren't there, and cards and calls poured in. Friends visited and gave freely of their time and self to stay with me. April had been working on starting a fund raising effort when I was called for the transplant; even friends, neighbors and co-workers of my friends contributed to that fund and to the blood drive that she coordinated. Anyone she knew or came in contact with she asked them for their blood. So many people I have yet to meet supported me. I know how fortunate I am.

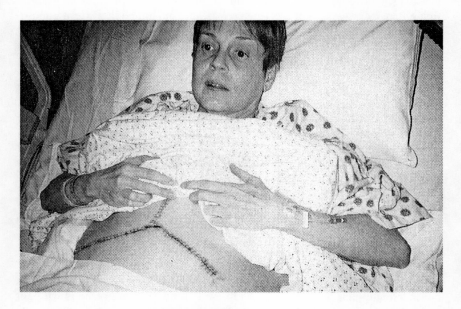

The "Mercedes" Scar

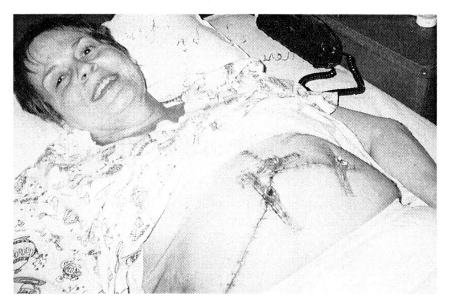

The Derailed Train Track

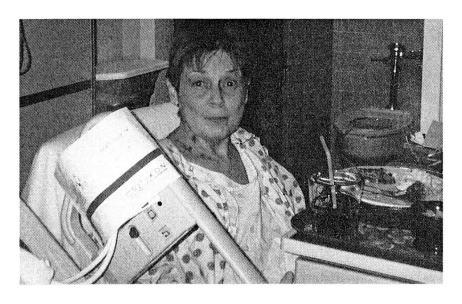

Almost There, November 2000

Barba Covington McCarty

20. Recovery

...And the Lord will wipe away tears from all faces...
Isaiah 25:8

I had not seen, or known I had seen, young Dr. Ernesto Molmenti who performed my transplant surgery, but my sisters and all my friends met him when he came out and gave them reports as the surgery progressed and when it ended. They were discussing his good looks, something I had no interest in. Later, I teased them that I was afraid they might try to get a transplant just to get too see him again. They jumped at the chance.

Dr. Molmenti showed up tall, dark-haired with a wide white smile looking like he had just put on a fresh, perfect body from the on-campus Tom Landry Center. He kept his professional composure around a room full of middle-aged women, most of whom were almost old enough to be his mother. The first day he came when Phyllis, Sherri or April wasn't there, he asked in his suave Argentinean accent where were my three friends. I was worried. What had they done that he remembered them? I'm still curious.

You will be encouraged to cough and do breathing exercises to keep your lungs clear and expanded to prevent pneumonia.

I took along a portable room air cleaner to use for "white noise" as I am a light sleeper and having been hospitalized before I knew that hospitals are not the best place to get sleep.

You are instructed to get out of bed very soon after going to a room from ICU, and a physical therapist will come by twice daily to work with you to help you regain your strength. Your routine is started very slowly, with exercises primarily for the thighs, which are very weak after a liver transplant. Because my strength was so non-existent before surgery, I did the exercises without the therapist there twice more daily. I was determined to get better ASAP. I walked extra times during the day or night if I was awake. After a few middle-of-the-night-strolls it was noted on my chart. Soon the doctor insisted that I was doing enough walking that I needed to rest and sleep some too.

After liver transplant, tremors are a problem thus making writing almost illegible. For someone like myself who was taking notes for later, it was a big disappointment. During this period, many of the notes I wrote are totally unreadable and many words are left out, but I have managed to recover most of them.

My new liver reacted sluggishly for a while; transplanted livers often do. The organ being on ice for a period of time causes this.

Your diet will be clear liquids, and you will progress to solid food. I had no appetite for food and spent time with every dietician available, trying to find out what I would eat. I was the exception; every transplant patient in BUMC when I was, said they wanted food very soon after receiving steroids. I, on the other hand, was still losing weight when I was dismissed to come home at three-and-a-half months post transplant, and it wasn't until after I had been home a few weeks (at almost five months post transplant) that I got hungry with a vengeance. I do things with a passion, or I don't do them at all, and this I did with an unsurpassed passion and will talk about in detail later in this book

October 13, my seventh day post transplant I wrote in my notes: I might get to go home Monday or Tuesday.

I didn't.

On October 15, I experienced a step backwards. I never expected that my worst pain after transplant would be fear. I tried to speak, and out came a jumbled muddle of slur, not words. Later, when a longtime friend called and wanted to talk to me (I wanted to talk to him as well) it was very frustrating for both of us when he could not understand one word I said. After an MRI, the medical team consistently referred to it as "damage," their double-talk word used to describe a stroke. Doctors told us it was caused by the first antirejection medication therapy I received.

Not only did the doctors avoid using the word stroke, I avoided it as well. Since I knew damage meant stroke, I was scared to leave the hospital, a problem that took care of itself since I experienced further complications that kept me there.

My friends and sisters did not question the word *damage* being used in place of stroke. Even though I knew what it meant, I dared not say it (even if I could have). I didn't utter or write the word *stroke*—even in my notes because others read them at the hospital—until after I was dismissed and home, and even then months later, because that word stroke would have wrecked havoc in the camp. Fear levels of my friends and family would have risen even higher than they were and telephones would have jangled non-stop. My sisters might have gotten out that pink coffin.

Speech therapists came and worked with me daily after the damage occurred. Every day after they left, I practiced the alphabet aloud in my room with emphasis on exaggerated vowels. I said aloud numbers 1 through 100 and the names of friends and family members in my husband's family and mine. My speech was not only very hard to understand it was hard for me to speak at all. I was horrified that I would not be understood when I spoke. During this time my speech could not be understood and my writing could not be read. Communication was terribly difficult so I mostly refrained from it.

Believe me, it took quite a bit of struggling through speech therapy before I realized that it was a miracle for my brain to be intact; I still had full use of my limbs and was not in a wheelchair or worse. I could care for myself, and I could still feed myself. Boy, can I feed myself while I am on steroids!

What did I get from that stroke? I already had a country Texas accent. Now I have a choppy, country Texas accent.

Whether your miracle happens so fast, like the car accident when my neck was broken, that you don't realize until later that it was a miracle, or if it is something you turned over to God and waited for, like I did for the transplant, or if it is like the stroke I had after the transplant when I didn't realize for quite a long time that it was miracle—when it's a miracle you know it.

I experienced another step backwards in the form of rejection. The body's normal response to defend itself against anything foreign is done through rejection. Rejections are anticipated, treated and reversible in most cases.

I had my plan to be dismissed and go to Twice Blessed House, my apartment home for the next three months, interrupted once already by the stroke when my recovery was abruptly interrupted again. This time the cause was acute rejection, a common occurrence. When a patient receives an organ transplant, the body's white cells will try to get rid of (reject) the transplanted organ. In spite of the drugs there is still a 60 percent to 70 percent chance of rejection. Rejection medications work by preventing the white cells from recognizing a new organ as foreign. Lymphocytes are a type of white blood cell. The lymphocytes involved in preventing the white cells from recognizing a new organ as foreign are B cells and T cells. B cells protect you against bacteria and T cells protect you from viruses, fungus, tumors and foreign tissues that enter your body. T cells are the soldiers of the immune system.

Two days after the "damage" first appeared, on October 17, 2000, while on team rounds, Dr. Molmenti informed me that I was rejecting and treatment would be IV steroids for five days.

Yet another step backwards came on October 24th. After the five days of IV steroids on October 24th. I was still rejecting and could not be dismissed. The treatment decided upon was muromonab-CD3 or Orthoclone OKT3, for simplicity sake known as OKT3, used to reduce the body's natural immunity in patients who receive organ transplants. OKT3 works by preventing the white blood cells from doing their job. OKT3 was begun immediately after some lab work. I had not heard about OKT3 beforehand. There may be a reason it is such a guarded secret. I never expected the treatment for rejection to make me feel worse than the transplant surgery. Dr. Molmenti told me I would feel bad with flu-like symptoms. My conclusion is, since I know Dr. Molmenti would not lie to me, that one of us, Dr. Molmenti or I, has not had the flu. He never once mentioned that not only would my fingers hurt and get stiff but that my fingernails would hurt, and I would feel too bad to cry. I had fever and chills; shaking under the cover chills.

More steps backwards—giant steps—came on October 24 – 27, 2000. I was moved to ICU almost immediately after OKT3 was started. My blood pressure dropped or rose I have forgotten which. My condition was almost immediately known, as vital statistics are taken every fifteen minutes, and if complications occur it is usually shortly after the first dose of OKT3. OKT3 was stopped while I was stabilized, and begun again, making the hoped-for average seven days of treatment turn into ten days of treatment for me.

Transplant patients form an enormous bond with the nurses who care for them. All the nurses were more than wonderful while I was on 14 Roberts and while I was in ICU. I fondly remember Rose Marie and Richard in ICU. However, there was a nurse, Sayda Majors, who was far beyond understanding. If there was a problem Sayda knew when I knew, often before I told her. Telling the nurses was extra hard, as I had already had the stroke and could barely be understood and talking was difficult. Sayda was more than just knowledgeable, and I mentioned that to her before I left ICU. Her mother-in-law had undergone a liver transplant, and is one of the people who have stood in my boots, that I mention later in this writing.

When I got out of ICU the second time I started running backwards. Second surgeries because of bleeding, are not uncommon for liver transplant patients. Soon after the acute rejection, my recovery was interrupted once again. I had big plans again to go to my apartment at Twice Blessed House. In fact, I had packed up all that I had gathered in the hospital room after staying there for several weeks when Dr. Levy pushed open the door to my room. I was lying on top of the cover, dressed and ready to go, complete with my New Balance tennis shoes on. Instead of his usual "How are you Honey?" he said, "You're not going to want to hear this…but, we're going to have to go in there again." I thought he was teasing and I replied with, "No, *we're* not." When I realized he wasn't teasing, I grabbed his arm and burst into tears with the whole team watching quietly around the walls of my room.

I wasn't bleeding but there was a "kink" in my hepatic artery, for whatever reason, which had to be repaired. Although, not too keen on the idea of another surgery, I wanted to be sure I was fixed before I left the hospital. One transplant is enough of a motivation to convince oneself that the doctors really do know best. Dr. Klintmalm did the surgery to repair the kink. The cut was the same; the old Mercedes scar was a blueprint for the new one, and all twenty inches of cut were stapled once again. This time I had three pieces of plastic ware attached to hold it together. Three ½-by-3-inch plastic pieces were held together with something that looked like fishing line or plastic thread. It looked somewhat like a derailed train track on my belly and aggravated me immensely. When the derailed train track came undone in one place, near time to remove it, my sister Betty and I removed it and told the doctor at clinic the following Friday.

The procedure, not exactly fun, was more tolerable than I imagined. However, the second surgery incision was sorer than the first but the recovery was quicker.

I had another backwards step when my bile duct stopped up. A stent was installed by Dr. Goldstein to open the duct for proper drainage.

By then, I felt I was waiting on death row, but at the same time, I felt there would be a successful outcome as all the others had been. I totally trusted Baylor's team of surgeons, anesthesiologist and nurses.

Somewhere, while running speedily backwards, I got Methicillin Resist Staphylococcus Aureas, MRSA, resistant bacteria that cannot be killed with antibiotics of the Penicillin family. From then on, I was isolated for any following hospitalizations for a period of two years. Now every time I am admitted to the hospital I am admitted into isolation and dismissed with my own red stethoscope and thermometer that I can carry home with me. So, after disinfecting with alcohol, all the kids I know have red stethoscopes to play doctor with.

The biopsy showed the OKT3 had worked. Just as I thought I was never going to see my apartment that my sisters and friends had seen and were all talking about, I was discharged from the newly remodeled room 1427 on November 3, 2000—day #29. Beverly, Betty and my brother-in-law, Loyd, moved me from the hospital to my apartment in the rain. I was home, well sort of. I did not know it then but the median stay after transplant is ten days.

Had I realized at the time that I was running speedily backwards, I might have been horrified, but I had complete confidence and trust in my doctors at Baylor. So, I had serenity to last until I got out of there. I did not want to go home until there was no doubt that I was ready. As a patient, I had patience.

Although it may seem like it, I do not think I *just won't die*; I am keenly aware that God does say no.

While still hospitalized, I managed to fit in four, I think, angiogram procedures and four of the six biopsies I have had. After I was dismissed, I had yet another angiogram. The angiograms were most uncomfortable afterwards, when I was clamped in a huge C clamp that I would swear was from James's garage, down at the groin area, twisted down and left to wait forty-five minutes or so to prevent bleeding. I did it without complaint. As I have said before, it's better to have the air as clear as possible especially where the word *bleeding* is mentioned as the reason.

When you are at your sickest fear abates; it is beat down, and off, by "feel badness." When I was so very ill before transplant and when all these backward steps were happening after transplant my fear level decreased. I constantly thought, "It's going to be all right, whatever all right is." It is a combination of busyness with what is at hand and abated fear. Abated fear; it is one of God's miracles in serious illness.

21. Twice Blessed

Twice Blessed House, appropriately named because we are truly twice blessed, is one of the greatest services Baylor has for transplant patients. It is located close to the Medical Center and is a housing complex specifically designed for patients and their families. There is a helpful and knowledgeable office staff on hand—who could ever forget Theresa Roberson who *knows everything* we need to know while we live there? Each apartment is fully furnished, including a washer and dryer, kitchen cookware and dishes, bed and bath linens, a vacuum cleaner and mop, a telephone and mail delivery with security provided. Being able to live near the hospital, have covered parking and access to shuttle service for frequent trips to the hospital provided by Baylor security for the three months I lived there, was a godsend.

There are many events scheduled to fill recovering patient's days; movie night, weekly community suppers, grocery store trips, mall trips, and since I was there during the Christmas season, there were Christmas light tours. There are videos and books to check out and a common room where other residents were usually there to talk with. I stayed so very busy with trips to the hospital, X-ray and lab, cleaning a drain that I still had, for some reason that I have forgotten, that I did not participate in any of the scheduled activities other than the Thursday evening community suppers. I was the exception but I did not know it then.

I found out later at the annual Baylor transplant reunion that other patients who were there when I was thought that I was not doing well at all. Some things are good not to know. I did know I was behind everyone else because of the doubly treated rejection, the stroke and the stent procedure, along with a drain tube procedure, all the angiograms and a second surgery. Still, I was too busy to know that I wasn't doing well and that everyone else wasn't having the many complications I was.

While I was hospitalized and recovering at Twice Blessed House, I had a serenity that I have never known before when I have had surgeries, injuries or fear. It's hard to know where that serenity comes from. I think it is a compilation of knowing I made it through the surgery and all the complications afterwards and knowing that if I were going to die it would have already happened. But, more than anything, I think it comes from the feeling of knowing it's all right whatever "all right" turned out to be. I have no idea exactly where that feeling comes from. I have talked to more people who did not have that feeling than those who did.

Ultimate Compassion

*You may not know me
But I know you and
Your ways of ultimate compassion.
This is not happenstance.*

*God planned my life
With this treasured possession
Given freely to me by you.
He planned your loved one's life too.*

*I am a representation
Of your departed loved one's being.
You offered me more than an organ;
You gave me life.*

*My thanks to you is countless.
And I shall treasure this gift
And care for it for what it is,
From an angel up above.*

Barba Covington McCarty
March 2001

22. My Donor's Family

Behold I send an Angel before you to keep you in the way ...
Exodus 23:20

I did not know that only ten percent of recipients ever meet or talk with their donor's family, so I *expected* to meet mine.

Writing an anonymous thank you letter to a donor family is emotional because you are alive due to of the loss of their loved one. It is frustrating because you have no idea why or how the donor died. All I knew of my donor was that he was a 51-year-old male, Caucasian. He may have been the victim of a stroke, aneurysm, drowning, asthma attack, accident, death by his own hand or murder, but whatever the reason for his death, I was alive because of it. What was shock and sorrow for the donor family was a miracle for me. Some recipients struggle with this issue. I did not struggle specifically with that issue because I had prepared myself during those long hours by meditating while playing tapes of the sounds of waterfalls when resting in bed and by praying for the family of whomever was going to be my donor. I knew they would have gone through the pain of losing a loved one who had suffered the unknown to most, brain death. I asked for prayer for my donor family in the Quivered Liver reports that I emailed to all my friends and family on the day the insurance company approved my transplant and on the thank-you notes I prepared to send to those who contributed to the fund April initiated and she and Phyllis were managing. I was not the reason for his death even though I live because of it. Some recipients after transplant feel an unjustified guilt; I have an immense swell of gratitude. I was made aware early in life, by my mother's death, that death is a part of living. It is the part that we all try to avoid for as long as we can but eventually God will say "come home" to all of us and no to our family members prayers.

God has said no to my family four times in four months and nine days, three of those times were within twenty-three days. This year, 2002, I have lost a sister and three nephews. I am very aware that I am the miracle in my family.

Donor families suffer much anguish after the brain death of a loved one, even without the added wondering of what happened to those who received their loved one's organs. Some want to know their loved one did "live on" as they hoped when they donated. Some families have gone years without ever hearing a word from someone they gave life to. Check the donor family message board at www.kidney.org.

Recipients are told only the age, sex and race of their donor but not the cause of his or her death.

Until I corresponded with and met some of Terry's family, I felt like a child who has an imaginary friend; one who provided comfort and security and was there when I needed him. I had never seen him, and he wasn't really there but, at the same time, he was so very real, so close, keeping me alive.

There are those people who do not write the donor family with the unknown cause of death of the donor so intense in their minds. Some people don't write because they have guilt; the recipient may feel they caused their disease that warranted a transplant with bad lifestyle choices. Some people don't write because they are not feeling well, and some people don't write because they are feeling so well after transplantation that they do not take the time to write a letter. Some actually feel guilty that they feel so well and the person whose organ that makes them feel so well is now gone. Some people have a fear that by bringing up their loved one's death the family may be needlessly upset again. Many people say, "I don't know what to say."

If you are the type who is at a loss for words a simple thank-you card with your first name signed at the bottom will suffice. But, if you choose to write a letter, tell them how your life has changed because of the transplant of the organ so freely given to you. Tell them what has happened in your life that might not have happened or what you would have missed without their generosity. If it were your loved one whose organs you donated to a very ill, unknown person, wouldn't you be curious to know how the person's life you saved is helped? If your loved one died by taking his or her own life, and your intention at his or her death was to see to it that his or her life "meant something," it would be so important to know that it did.

The recipient's family members may write letters to the donor family too. I am aware of one donor family who received a letter from one of their son's recipients and four letters from the recipient's relatives. They were ecstatic.

To those who do not write to the donor family, I ask: Why? They *gave* you the gift of life. Being silently grateful is not enough. Being vocally grateful to others is not enough. Say thank you to the donor family. Even though it may not seem like enough, and it won't; it is true there are no words for the thank you we should say but those two words are the only ones we have. When I sat down to write my thank-you letter I thought to myself *I can convey to them how grateful I am, I am a writer.* I will dress it up and make them know how thankful I am for the life they gave me by giving me *a part of their loved one.* Many rewrites later the only words there was to say how grateful and thankful I am were thank you. The donor family was selfless and thought of others in a time of great grief and sorrow. There is no reason whatsoever when a thank-you letter, card or note should not be written and mailed to the donor family through the anonymous process we have available to us. The fact that the transplant occurred years ago is not a reason not to write them; donor families never quit wondering about the recipients of their loved one. To the donor family, a recipient did not receive an organ they received part of their loved one; if it was a child, spouse or sibling that donor was a part of the family he or she left behind.

The donor family may not respond to your thank-you letter as mine did. Unlike a recipient, there is really no need for them to unless it is their desire; they did not receive, they gave, you received. I have met recipients who say they are scared to meet their donor family. I am so glad mine did respond, and I have met some members of his family.

I have found that donor families are sometimes not aware that they can send a letter to recipients or their families, even if they have not received a letter from the recipient, by the anonymous process administered through the organ bank that assisted them at the time of donation. More often than not, we as recipients are not told how our donor died, therefore all recipients wonder.

If you wish to stay in contact, say so in your letter. Remember the process for a letter to get to someone takes over a month even if there are no changes of addresses or other red tape in the lives of whoever is receiving the letter. And, a reply from them takes over another month also, or they may hold your letter and not respond for a while. It's up to the donor family, and it should be; they gave us our lives. They are allowed however long it takes to write back, and they are allowed not to write back at all if that is their wish.

The following is what I wrote in my thank you letter to the people who made the decision that saved my life:

Barba

February 2, 2001

Hello,

I am very sorry for the loss of your loved one. I have prayed for you daily and will continue to do so.

I am writing to say thank you for the unique gifts you have given me, my life and my health. You bless me daily.

By nature, I am an optimistic person, so dying was not an option for me; however, I was afraid that I might not make it through the long wait. Then, when the results of my pre-transplant evaluation revealed me to be the rare B-positive blood type I was even more afraid that the wait would take too long.

I had been ill for so long with my dysfunctioning liver that I had forgotten what feeling good was like. I was too sick to want to eat and had forgotten the simple thing of how food is supposed to taste when it's good. In fact, I am going to have to watch this newfound taste I have.

My entire life is changed and is much better since my transplant. I walk a mile and a half now... without stopping. I didn't go to Wal-Mart before my liver transplant because the store was too big. By the time I got inside the store from the parking lot, I was already tired. You have no idea how many times I left food stores before I was finished buying groceries because I was too weak and tired to finish the job. The diseased liver ran my life.

I am about to celebrate another birthday that I very well might not have celebrated without your caring and generosity.

I realize that, in the future, should you ever want to meet or talk to me the choice is yours. If you do, I will be here for you.

The two words, *thank you,* seem not to be enough. Please accept them from the bottom of my heart, near my liver.

God bless you,
Barba

* * *

On April 9, 2001, I went to the mailbox and found a letter from Baylor UMC. As I receive many letters from Baylor, I was not suspicious or curious about its contents. When I got back inside, I opened the envelope. I noticed the letter was handwritten and on stationery with yellow roses in the upper left-hand corner. The date in the upper right-hand corner was March 2, 2001. To myself I wondered why it took so long, five weeks, in arriving. I started to read. "Barba, my name is Nancy. I received your letter, and it was such a blessing to hear from you. I sat and cried for an hour or more after reading your letter…"

It hit me. *The letter was from someone in my donor's family.* I started to cry and couldn't see to read the letter through my tears. I was in a hurry to get to the end of the letter, and when I did, I cried some more and read it over several times.

I called Phyllis who didn't answer the phone. In my excitement about getting the letter, even after receiving no answer on her phone, I immediately got in my car and drove, crying all the way, the twenty-two miles to her house to show her my letter. At her house I got out of the car and ran, yes, I could run again, to the backdoor. It was locked; she wasn't outside where she didn't hear the phone ring. She really wasn't home. I was crying with joy and frustrated that Phyllis wasn't home. I started back to the car when her husband, W.H., yelled to me while walking from his workshop at the back of the house. I couldn't say anything for crying so when he reached me at the back porch I handed the letter to him, and he read it while I cried and I tried to cry silently but couldn't. In my return letter from my donor's widow, she told me that her husband bred and raised Pomeranian dogs and how proud he was of them. Because I have a general dislike for dogs, and I am also allergic to them, when W.H. finished reading the letter I boohooed, "How am I going to tell Nancy I don't like dogs?"

Nancy was my donor's widow. In the letter she expressed a desire to keep in touch with me, and she told me she worked at a hospital in Athens and signed her first and last names, Nancy Sharp. Since she had indicated in the letter that she wanted contact, without a doubt, I felt I could locate her from the information she had provided in the letter.

So when I got home, I got on the computer to look for a phone number listed for her. When I didn't find one listed in her name, naturally, I checked for one in the name of her husband but that failed also. So I began to try to locate the cities around Cedar Creek Lake where she told me she lived but did not list the city. There was something like sixteen communities that surrounded the lake with a population of a big city. I found a link to newspapers in the Cedar Creek Lake area and entered her last name, Sharp, in the computer search bar, thinking an ad for Pomeranian dogs might appear with a phone number but what appeared was an obituary for Terry Sharp, my donor. Alone, I cried and read it over and over again by the light of my computer screen. Then, I emailed a copy of the obituary to my longtime friend April, and when she got home from work, I called her. We emailed back and forth after the telephone call with short messages and questions. I had not realized it, but April noticed from information in the obituary in the newspaper that I had received the letter from Nancy on Terry's birthday, April 9th, and pointed it out to me that it would be a sad day for his family that day.

I kept searching the Internet and went to Yahoo Yellow Pages and located the hospital in the city where Nancy had told me she worked. I dialed the number hesitantly, because I was afraid I would get her and possibly upset her at work. So, I set out just to find out what floor she worked on so I could send her another letter to avoid the over two months it had taken for the letters to go through the proper anonymous channels available to us. It was nighttime, and I really thought to find out what I wanted to know I'd have to call back during the day. I said to the woman who answered the phone, "I need to speak to Nancy Sharp; she works there but I don't know where she works." The switchboard operator informed me that she did not know her but she could ring "the second floor, and if she doesn't work there, get them to ring first." I said, "Well, this could take a while, how many floors do y'all have?" She said, "Two." We laughed. Then, forgetting my goal to find out only where Nancy worked, I said, "Ring me to second."

Someone answered on the second floor, and I asked for Nancy Sharp. If the person who answered said, "Just a minute," like she was going to get Nancy, I had planned to hang up and write a letter and send it to the second floor of the hospital. But, the woman who answered said, "She's not here today." I was stunned. She knew her. She worked there.

After a pause, I asked, "But...she works in there?"

"Yes Ma'am," and again, "but she's not here today."

"When will she be there?"

"I don't know when she'll be back. I don't know if this is her first night off or what."

Then I asked again, "She works in there where you are though?"

Once again, in a less patient voice she said, "Yes Ma'am, but she off today."

I asked her if she would call Nancy and give her my number and ask her to call me. The lady said she didn't know Nancy's number or even where she lived and added that Nancy was fairly new working there. I tried another route by asking if they had access to email at work and received, yet, another no reply.

I said, "Can you hold on just for a minute? I need to think this out." I was stalling I hadn't planned on this happening. Then I asked, "Is there a place where you can leave her a note that she will see?"

Of course, her reply was, "Yes Ma'am."

I told her to put on the note that Barba called and to add my phone number. Then I really got under the nice woman's skin. I knew that Nancy would have noticed the spelling of my name in script at the top of the letter I had mailed to my donor family; everybody thinks it's misspelled, so I asked her how she had spelled Barba. She said, "How do you want me to spell it?" I instructed her in the spelling of my name as *Barba*, not Barbara or Barbra. Then she asked me how to spell McCarty. She had been more than patient with me, so I indulged her in the spelling of my last name that is also frequently misspelled as McCarthy, but I knew Nancy did not have my last name. We checked the telephone number for accuracy. I thanked her and we hung up.

It was about 8 PM when I called the hospital, so I thought that apparently Nancy worked the evening shift. The next day I stayed home after 3 o'clock and waited for her to get my message and possibly call me. I stayed home the next morning in case she waited to call me from home and not from work. Near noon I gave myself a good talking to about sitting and waiting for her to call; she might not have even gotten my message. She might be off for a week or more or on one of those shifts where some nurses do all weekend work. I put it out of my mind and ran around most of the afternoon. Later as I sat at my computer writing, just after 7 PM, my phone rang. A lady with a really slow Texas drawl said, "Bar...ba, this is Nan...cy Sharp. I got your message." I was speechless, almost. She said she wanted me to know she had gotten to work and received my message. We exchanged phone numbers and decided to talk later when she was at home the next day. Just before we hung up Nancy asked, "Oh, where are you calling from?"

I replied, "Paris."

She said, "Oh... Paris, well... I have a sister who lives in Reno."

I replied, "Reno city limits is about two blocks around the corner from me." She told me her sister's name. I didn't know her.

The next day, April 11, 2001, as I waited until the time we had agreed upon for me to call Nancy, my phone rang. It was Nancy calling me.

We talked forty-five minutes, and she told me about her husband and about the fall morning in October when he awoke with a terrible headache and had put their morning coffee on as he did every morning. As part of their daily ritual; she would get dressed and come by the coffee pot he had filled and turned on, she'd fill two cups with coffee and carry them into where he would be sitting to talk to her while enjoying their morning coffee. But, on this morning instead of Terry sitting in his chair waiting for the coffee he was lying on the sofa holding his head. When she asked him what was wrong, he said he had a terrible headache. She insisted on calling the doctor, but he said no that he wasn't calling the doctor with a headache. About that time, they saw one of Terry's dogs had escaped the pen and ran across the yard. She told Terry to get back in bed, that she would chase the dog down and put him back in the pen, then she would return and make him an ice pack for his headache. Nancy started for the door, and Terry started down the hallway to the bedroom when she heard a loud thud. She knew he had fallen and rushed to him. She told me how she had no idea how she did it but that she picked him up and put him on the bed and called 911.

She told me they had been married nearly six years and about their children; both of them had children from previous marriages, and I told her I had none. I gave her a brief story about my life in general and we decided that we would meet in Paris since her sister lived here and Nancy's son had recently gotten out of service and hadn't seen his aunt and cousins since his return. Before hanging up the phone, we agreed she would call me when she reached her sister's house on the weekend of April 21, 2001. We did not agree on a time she would call and she didn't even know which day of the weekend she was coming.

* * *

When Nancy and her son arrived at her sister's house, her sister's family was about to go eat at the Fish Fry Restaurant where they had a reservation. Nancy called me to see if I would like to tag along. I was a bit apprehensive about meeting her in a public place, because I knew it would be an emotional meeting for both of us. But, she said, "Well, we'll meet in the lobby before we go in, won't we?" I agreed, knowing at 6:45 PM on a Saturday the lobby of the Fish Fry is always full of people. It was 6:30 PM when she called, so I wore what I had on and got in my Buick, thinking since I lived very close to the Fish Fry that I would beat them there and stand outside in the foyer and wait for them as I looked for the teddy bears that she had described to me that were on her shirt. On the way inside, just outside the door, I passed two young men who were standing looking around as if they were looking for someone. I wondered if one of them might be Nancy's son but dismissed the idea since he was with another young man and not with a lady with teddy bears on her shirt. I peeked inside the filled lobby and just as I decided they weren't in there and turned to go back to the foyer to wait a woman reached for my arm. She had teddy bears on her shirt. It was Nancy, one of the people who made the decision to save my life. We embraced and cried in the lobby of the Fish Fry; it was so crowded that no one else noticed.

Nancy introduced me to her sister and her sister's grown daughter along with a couple of small children that were with her sister. Then the two young men from outside came in; they were Nancy's son and her nephew. As we waited to be called for seating, I said to Nancy's sister that I thought I might know her, but I didn't. She said she'd thought the same and added, "But, I go to church right around the corner from where you live." I tried to think where there was a church right around the corner and didn't come up with one. She said, "That church right up on the loop behind the Belk store."

I was astonished and must surely have looked like I was. I attended that church, The United Pentecostal Church in Paris, Texas, as a little girl, almost forty years earlier when my mother was alive. I added, "I have been on the prayer list over there. I used to go to that church when I was little girl, and I have many old and dear friends who go to that church. You may have prayed for me."

Nancy's sister didn't answer right away. Suddenly she looked in awe and said, "You and Terry might have been on the prayer list at the same time." I couldn't find out; the church doesn't keep a written prayer list in the church bulletin like some churches do, they have a prayer circle.

Nancy came home with me from the Fish Fry and we talked until after 11 PM when I took her to her sister's house for the night.

We talked about the time Terry spent in the hospital after he had what at first appeared to be a stroke. October 3rd he was taken to a hospital in Athens, near where they lived, and was later transferred to a Tyler hospital. It wasn't until a doctor asked her if Terry had sustained a blow to the head that the accident three days earlier with the back door of his SUV falling and hitting his head entered her mind. As close as it could be determined the accident with the car door had caused an aneurysm to form, and he later lost his life because of a hit on the head. The family was told he was brain dead. They got second opinions that confirmed the diagnosis, and he was pronounced dead on October 5, 2001. The family held a gathering and made the decision of ultimate compassion to donate his organs.

Nancy gave me a picture of she and her husband, *my donor of life*; I had wondered so often how he looked. Terry was a tall man, very slim with black hair, exactly the opposite of me. I am a short woman, definitely not slim with blond hair. Suddenly—tall and short, man and woman, slim and fat, black hair and blond and yes, dead and alive—Terry and Barba became the same to me.

Nancy has since heard from another of Terry's recipients, a lady who received one of his kidneys. I thought she might have been living at Twice Blessed House, recuperating also, when I was, and we were unaware that we shared life by the same donor. I kept a telephone sheet from the time I lived at the apartment complex; there is no one listed with her first name, which is all Nancy has from her letter. Possibly, she lived close enough to Baylor not to have to live at the apartment complex; or possibly she lives in the area of Ft. Worth, which is in another organ procurement area; or maybe she lives down by Galveston, father away but in the same procurement area as Dallas; or in an area far, far away where she was critical and was first on the list.

Nancy has written her back and is hoping she will reply again as I do. I feel a strange connection to the other recipient.

* * *

He did not know what took place through the angel was real...
Acts 12:9

23. It's a Small, Small, Small World

An unplanned sudden meeting that came with sweet surprise...
From a poem by Barba McCarty, *Friend That I Love*

I n Dallas, ex co-workers, Ticha Hamilton and Jacky Mathews, along with a friend and neighbor of Jacky's, Tommy Welch and Ticha's husband, Derek Hamilton, planned to attend a Sandi Patty concert to raise funds for Reaching America's Youth. Ticha, Jacky and Tommy attended the concert. Ticha's husband, Derek was absent. It was October 6, 2000.

Jacky, who has been a Sandi Patty fan since 1983 when he attended a Billy Graham Crusade with his church group at the age of thirteen, wanted to try to get front row seats, so Ticha arrived at Jacky's apartment at 5:30 PM so they could get to the concert early. She didn't elaborate but explained her husband's absence by saying that he wouldn't be attending because his uncle was hospitalized.

As Jacky drove to the concert and Ticha applied her makeup in the front passenger seat, Tommy sat in the backseat and said, "Jacky, remember my friend Barba that I told you about that is waiting for a liver transplant? April said she got a call last night; she has a donor."

Ticha's interest peaked in the conversation about Tommy's friend waiting for a liver transplant, and she told them that Derek's family had made the decision to donate his uncle's organs. During the conversation Tommy mentioned that his friend Barba had a rare blood type. As they rode to the concert, Tommy and Ticha questioned each other and decided that Tommy's friend might possibly be the recipient of the donated liver of Derek's uncle.

* * *

On April 9, 2001, six months and three days after my transplant, I got a reply to my thank-you letter to my donor's family, and shortly after, I met my donor's widow, Nancy. I was stirred emotionally and thrilled to have met Nancy and wanted to share the news with my family and friends. I composed and sent the same email, good news instead of a quivered liver report, to all my online family and friends, some I have known since grade school and high school, telling them I had met my donor's widow and her sister who lived so close to me and attended the church I had attended when I was a young girl. I ended the email with, "Her name is Nancy. Isn't it a small world?" For my donor's widow's privacy I used only her first name.

I got replies from all my online friends but one, Tommy Welch, who when he received the email, remembered the conversation he had with Ticha on the night of the Sandi Patty concert. As his interest peaked, he sent an email to his friend, Jacky asking him if the wife of Derek's uncle was named Nancy, then he left to go out of town on a business trip. When Tommy returned from his business trip, he had a reply to the question he had asked Jacky via email; yes, her name was Nancy Sharp.

Tommy sent a one-sentence email to me: "If your donor's wife's name is Nancy Sharp, I have something to tell you in the small world department." I knew it was something good because he had Nancy's last name; I had not given her last name in the email I sent to friends. I couldn't wait the time it takes to send an email and possibly not get a quick reply, so I tried to call Tommy but that failed; his area code had changed. So, I sent an email to him saying yes her name was Nancy Sharp and anxiously waited over an hour. I checked the telephone number I had for Tommy and finally reached him when the operator told me his area code had changed. He told me about going to the concert with his friend, Jacky, and Jacky's ex-coworker, Ticha, whose husband was with his family. Tommy didn't even remember Ticha's last name; he knew her husband was Derek; they lived in Mesquite, Texas and had two small children.

I got out the copy of Terry's obituary I had found online the night I received Nancy's letter and saw there was a surviving sister who lived in Mesquite.

This accidental, but seemingly planned, event led me to my donor's genetic family.

* * *

Six more months later, in October 2002, when I was hospitalized for rejection, my dear friend April, who attended high school with Tommy and me, began the proverbial grapevine once again. This communication is responsible for my meeting Terry's genetic family; April told Tommy, via email, that I was hospitalized; Tommy mentioned it to Jacky and Jacky to Ticha who passed along the news to her husband, Derek Hamilton, my donor's nephew.

Derek visited me in the hospital. He arrived at my hospital room door on his lunch hour with a *Cosmopolitan* magazine, a *People* magazine, a bottle of Clairol Herbal Essences lotion and a beautiful card tucked inside a gift bag. We talked about his uncle, who Derek said had a fondness for fishing. I had wondered if my donor smoked and had forgotten to ask Nancy. Derek said his uncle might smoke a cigar occasionally while out fishing, but no, he otherwise did not smoke. Derek wondered about stories he had heard about recipients taking on some the characteristics of donors, and wanted to know if my tastes or anything like that had changed. I told him I had no idea; I liked no foods before, but now I was on steroids, and I liked everything!

Derek informed me that another of his uncles was going to be having surgery the next day in Dallas where I was hospitalized, and his mother and her sister would be in town for that surgery the next day, and they might drop by if that was all right. I said it was. We exchanged addresses and Derek left.

Somehow I didn't expect Derek's mother and her sister because it was the anniversary of their brother's death, and I was hospitalized for rejection of his liver. I understood how painful it would be for Terry's sisters to meet me at that time and under the circumstances that I was hospitalized. They didn't come by the hospital.

At Christmas, I received a card from Derek and Ticha with a note enclosed saying Derek's mother, Terry's sister, wanted to meet me, and if I was ever in the Dallas area, would I contact them and try to get together with them. That happened in Dallas on March 15, 2002.

It was so special to meet the people who made the decision that saved my life. I had tried to imagine what Terry's sister looked like, and she looked exactly as I thought she would; tall and slender with dark hair, very much like Terry in the picture that Nancy had given me.

Barba Covington McCarty

24. Other Angels

...no matter what you call it
it didn't come without design,
For all our lives are fashioned
By the Hand That Is Divine.
Helen Steiner Rice, from a poem, Not by Chance or Happenstance

There is one reason that all transplant recipients are alive, and that reason is that there are angels out there who have the ultimate compassion in their time of greatest sorrow to give so freely the gift of life to those waiting for life-saving organs.

In this writing I have used the phrase "dying was not an option for me" to let you know my intensity for living, but in reality that option was not mine. That option belongs to donor families. There are other angels out there with my donor and his family, who are my family of angels, and below are the stories of some of those other angels I have had the privilege to know their family members, who have so graciously shared their stories with me to share with you.

I met donor mom, Beverly Carroll, who is allowing me to tell her story, when I attended a Southwest Transplant Alliance volunteer training session in Dallas. I met the other donor moms when I volunteered to assist them in writing letters to their son's recipients. Each donor family has a unique story and unique feelings about why they donated the organs of their loved ones, but every one of them share the same desire to hear from the recipients.

In Honor of Kelly Michele Harris
April 4, 1963 to June 11, 1986
Donor Mom, Beverly Carroll

On June 6, 1986, Beverly Carroll and her husband were moving into their dream house in Houston, Texas and had went to bed tired from moving all day.

When the downstairs phone rang at 3 AM Beverly was concerned, because only two people had the new number, her two daughters, Kelly, 23, and Lori, 21. Beverly almost fell while rushing down the stairs in a new environment to find the phone she had forgotten where she had plugged in. By the time she reached the phone, it had quit ringing. She worried about the phone ringing at that time of night and moved it to another phone jack upstairs closer to where she and her husband were sleeping. She found it hard to get back asleep but finally dozed off when the phone rang again. This time, when she answered the phone a policeman asked her if she had a son named Kelly. She told him no, but she had a daughter named Kelly; Beverly's phone number had been found in Kelly's wallet. The policeman informed her that Kelly and Lori had been in a terrible car accident along with two other young women, friends of Kelly's she had not seen in a long time, and that she needed to come to Dallas, Texas to RHD hospital as soon as possible. Stunned and in shock she hung up the phone and was crying when it rang again. This time the voice on the other end of the phone line was that of a doctor at RHD hospital in Dallas telling her that her daughter Kelly was in critical condition and was in surgery. Her daughter Lori was admitted but not serious. The other two women had walked away uninjured.

Beverly and her husband's clothes were thirty-five miles away at their old house, they were in Houston and their injured daughters were hospitalized in Dallas. By the time Beverly and her husband caught a plane and reached Dallas it was 8:30 in the morning.

When they arrived Kelly was still in surgery with massive head injuries sustained after a young man driving exceedingly fast slammed into the back of the car. Kelly had been thrown from the back seat of a Chevy hatchback, where she and her sister were riding without their seatbelts fastened.

Other than one stitch on the end of her index finger, Kelly had no injuries from her shoulders down; she was a perfect donor, her mother said. Beverly did not believe her daughter would die and Kelly was kept on life support for five days. On the fifth day, a doctor took the family in and told them there were no brain waves and that Kelly actually had died the night of the accident.

When the trained requestors from Southwest Transplant Alliance came to discuss donation of Kelly's organs with Beverly, there was no question in her mind that her precious, sensitive, daughter with the strawberry-colored hair, who wanted to be a veterinarian, would have wanted to donate to help others live. She said the first thought that came to her mind was that Kelly could live on in someone else. Her second thought was that Kelly would have been proud to know she could save someone's life. Beverly donated all of Kelly's organs and tissue and she feels lifted up just knowing so many other people benefited from Kelly's gifts.

In the years following Kelly's death Beverly thought of nothing but grief. She now wishes she had tried to contact or meet some of Kelly's recipients of life and those who's lives were enhanced by her gifts of tissue.

A few months ago, after attending a transplant gala and meeting other recipients, Beverly contacted Southwest Transplant Alliance to find out the condition of the recipients of Kelly's organs and tissue. She found out that Kelly's heart recipient has since been re-transplanted, and some of her recipients are no longer reachable through the agency. When she was told of the heart recipient having to be re-transplanted, she said she felt Kelly had died again because her heart is no longer beating inside someone else. But, she would still like to meet the man who received Kelly's heart even though he has another heart now.

A man from the Dallas area who got one of her kidneys has since passed away from causes unrelated to the transplant.

Beverly wishes she had tried to contact the recipients long ago. She has no doubt that several lives were saved and many were enhanced.

Beverly told me that writing her story to share with readers in this book helped her, but that even after sixteen years, she still wonders about the recipients she has never heard from. They include a man in Abilene who got the other kidney and a person who got Kelly's liver who was transplanted at Baylor University Medical Center and others.

She still has hope of hearing from them.

Beverly plans to write letters to the recipients and ask Southwest Transplant Alliance to send them to whatever address they have on file for each recipient. She has hopes that even after this long maybe some relative still lives at the address where the recipients lived sixteen years ago.

Beverly's is a case where it is still not too late to write a thank you letter to the donor family even after sixteen years. After all these years, she now lives in the Dallas area but has contacted the organ agency, Southwest Transplant Alliance. They have her address. She could receive the letters she so wants to receive.

In Honor of James B. Riley
March 11, 1976 – July 16, 1995
Donor Mom, Pearlie Wingate

Jamie Riley was a regular blood donor who loved fishing. He was a gentle soul who made friends easily and had many. His funeral was the biggest ever held by the funeral home that handled his final care. The funeral home had been in business for seventy-five years. Jamie had a soft spot in his heart for kids and cried for the children killed on the day of the Oklahoma City bombing which happened just three months before his death.

Jamie's family received a letter from one of his recipients and his mother, Pearlie, framed it and the Christmas card they received from another recipient. After she heard from the two men who received Jamie's kidneys, she sent them pictures of the dark-haired young man with a narrow face, big smile and an indention in his chin. When she heard from neither of them after she mailed the photos of Jamie, she wrote to the two men again, six-and-a-half years after Jamie's death. A month or so later, when she had not received replies, she inquired about their condition through the procurement agency that handled Jamie's donations and found out bad news; both men's kidneys were failing, one was in serious condition and the other was in critical. At the time of this writing, Pearlie feels she may never meet Jamie's recipients and is praying for a miracle for the two men. It may be that the two men will get a second kidney transplant that will save their lives again and possibly she can meet them. But no matter what happens, the two men lived at least seven extra years each because of Jamie's kidneys that his family so graciously donated.

At Jamie's death, he left his father, mother, two brothers, two sisters, two grandmothers and a host of friends who miss him.

On July 16, 1995, Jamie died at the age of nineteen, in his mother's backyard of a self-inflicted gunshot wound. She has had great sorrow and trouble coping with his death and after six-and-a-half years told his recipients how he died.

After his death, Pearlie was told Jamie was HCV positive and she worried that he had spread hepatitis through the blood donations he made, usually twice a year.

Blood donated after July 1992 was screened and not used and before that time there was no way to tell when blood was tainted with HCV, so any infection then was accidental and unavoidable but is often the reason for so many people having HCV, which years after the infection, leads to severe illness, transplant or death for many of them.

If Jamie was infected when he gave his blood donations, he had no way of knowing. If someone later is in need of a transplant after receiving his tainted blood it is because medical technology was not then what it is today. If that does happen Jamie has already paid in full for any transgression he unknowingly committed by adding at least seven years to the life of two others.

In Honor of Travis Munn
March 28, 1979 – March 11, 2001
Donor Mom, Jeanne Munn

Travis Munn dropped friends off and was two blocks from home when he lost control of his silver Mazda 626 that he cherished and hit a tree on the chilly spring morning of March 10, 2001, just two weeks short of his twenty-second birthday. To look at Travis in the trauma center, he looked almost perfect, no cuts or bruises, only a few scratches, but he was in serious condition. The following day, on March 11, 2001, their gentle spirited son, Travis, was pronounced brain dead following the car accident. When Jeanne and her husband Stewart were approached about organ donation at a Florida hospital they looked at each other and spontaneously said, "Yes."

Travis worked in the parts department at the local Toyota dealership and was saving his money to move out on his own when his life filled with so many friends ended abruptly.

Jeanne thinks things do not happen without reason, although sometimes we do not know the reason, in Travis' case she does know what the reason was. Jeanne believes it was so others could live and that it is all a part of God's plan. Donating Travis' organs makes her feel that they made a good contribution of life to several other people, among them, a forty-seven-year old man who suffered ischemic heart disease for ten years before he received Travis' heart; a sixty-six-year old retired teacher and grandmother of six who received Travis' liver as the second transplanted liver she had in less than a year; a thirty-eight-year old female who had suffered type 1 diabetes since the age of ten received his left kidney. She had been married only four years and could no longer do her favorite things like ride her horse. She had experienced a previous kidney transplant in 1992; the other kidney went to a thirty-seven-year-old man, a perfect match with Travis' kidney, who had Berger's Disease and had also experienced a previous kidney transplant in 1993. He had two young children and can now take them fishing, go to the gym and go diving.

I'm looking at Travis' picture now. It is hard to believe this smiling, clean-cut young man pictured above a tribute to him in the Munn's local newspaper is no longer living. He looks so alive.

Jeanne says it brings comfort to her family to know about the recipients and makes them aware that they did the right thing. They believe that Travis would have wanted his organs donated.

Travis' family has since heard from the recipient of his left kidney, the woman who had been afflicted with type 1 diabetes. When they received her letter, there were four more letters included from other members of her family. The bundle of five letters arrived in the Munn mailbox just before their first Christmas without Travis. Jeanne says the letters got them through Christmas. The Munn's have not heard from any of the other recipients.

In Honor of Scott Nester
December 22, 1975 – October 17, 2000
Donor Mom, Trish Nester

A group of eight young men from Auglaize County, Ohio, all in their twenties, went to ride the trails on farmland owned by a friend in Shelby County, Ohio, on an autumn Sunday afternoon. Among them was Scott Nester, 24, an avid photographer and collector of antique beer bottles from breweries in the area where he lived. He was riding a four-wheeler without a helmet. Scott tried to attempt to ride the 300cc Honda up a vertical creek bank, but as he neared the top, about fourteen feet above the creek bed, his ATV flipped over and landed on his head. He was taken to a local hospital then transferred by CareFlight helicopter to a Dayton, Ohio, hospital where he was pronounced brain dead two days later.

As the family waited at the hospital, hoping for a miracle that didn't come, his mother remembered a year earlier when Scott told her if anything ever happened to him, she should donate his organs because he wouldn't be needing them anymore. When Life Connection of Ohio approached her, she agreed to donate his organs to help Scott help others.

When I first connected with Trish Nester in June, eight months after her son's death in October, she was wondering how the recipients of Scott's organs were doing; she wanted to know if Scott's wish for someone to use his organs that he no longer needed was working.

Those receiving life from Scott were a twenty-four-year-old man from the Toledo area who had been on dialysis since high school because his kidneys failed after he had been taking insulin since the age of four, who received a lifesaving kidney and a pancreas transplant; a single forty-five-year-old man in the Dayton area who is rearing two boys received Scott's right kidney; and a forty-year-old man from Indiana who has a wife, two daughters and a son got a new liver.

Scott lived at home with his parents and a younger sister and worked at a company that makes forklifts. He was a man of many hobbies; in addition to collecting old beer bottles, he collected other things. He was a photographer and always carried his camera with him to capture interesting subjects like buildings that were about to be torn down so people in the future could see what their surroundings had once looked like. He enjoyed four-wheeling, trucks, cars and dirt bikes.

Scott, in the photo I have before me, along with three beautiful poems written in his honor by his mother, was a dark-haired young man with laughing eyes. I can imagine him on a four-wheeler, enjoying the struggle up a steep incline on a Sunday afternoon with a crowd of friends.

Trish has yet to hear from any of Scott's recipients; she is still waiting and hoping to hear from them.

Scott would be glad to know that he not only helped these three men, he saved their lives, so they could be with five children.

In Honor of Jacob Blastow
July 23, 1982 – December 1, 1998
Donor Mom, Phyllis Keith

Jacob loved basketball and dreamed about being a star. He was very smart with computers and won a college scholarship when he was in the ninth grade. He started playing darts when he was twelve.

Jacob worked at a super market and was a fun loving Tampa, Florida, high school student who took his own life at the age of sixteen.

When Jacob ended his life, he enhanced the lives of others, among them are twenty-two-year-old woman from Argentina who received one of his eyes; a sixty-eight-year-old man from the Jacksonville, Florida, area who received his other eye; and a thirteen-year-old girl who received bone and tendons. This girl would be about seventeen now, and Phyllis's hope is that she is enjoying a much fuller life and having carefree teenage years. A baby boy in Texas received a heart valve. Thirty-five bone grafts were used to enhance the lives of many others.

Jacob's solid organs could not be used because he suffered cardiac death instead of brain death.

The Irish Fox and Hounds, a pub in Brandon, Florida, where Jacob played darts, sponsors a memorial tournament every year around Jacob's birthday. The proceeds go to Life Link to help people who have no money pay for medicines.

Jacob's brother, James, and his wife, Tina, have since had a child. His name is Jacob Blastow, II.

It is important that his family know his donations helped the recipients, but they have not heard from any of them.

In Honor of Kenneth Patrick Lay
May 31,1985 – November 2, 2000
Donor Mom, Jamie Lay

Patrick, at age15, a ninth grade high school student was doing one of the things he liked best, riding his four-wheeler, when he was struck and killed by a speeding motorist in his hometown on a late autumn day.

Jamie tells me that the state did an alcohol and drug test on her son when he was killed but did not bother to do one on the man who hit him.

Patrick had a kind heart and many friends, several of whom he had invited to attend church with him the Sunday after he was killed. He was helpful to his mother and family and to their handicapped neighbors he checked on daily.

He signed a donor card when he got his learning driver's license permit just a few months before his death and made the whole family know he wanted to donate. Knowing that he wanted to donate made the decision easier for them when they were approached after he was declared brain dead. They know they did the right thing.

Patrick's family has heard nothing from any of his recipients. In March 2002, sixteen months after they would have received their transplants, Jamie wrote letters to all of them. It's been three months since she sent the letters, and she still has not heard from any of the recipients.

Patrick's family—three brothers, three sisters and his mom and dad— would like to know how the recipients are doing.

25. About Transplant

The time that it takes you to do a thoughtful and generous favor that wasn't
expected of you, the time that it takes just to answer the call...
The time that you take when you care.
From a poem by Amanda Bradley, *Friendship is Only A Matter of Time*

Two million deaths occur in the United States each year. Of those two million, twenty-two thousand are a result of brain death. Those figures mean Americans are almost ninety-one times as likely to die a cardiac death as they are to die of brain death.

Of those twenty-two thousand who do die of brain death, there are five thousand who are not medically suitable to become donors because of active core hepatitis B, metastasized cancer or HIV.

Liver transplantation, performed under general anesthesia, within twelve to twenty-four hours after surgical retrieval from a donor is considered to be the most difficult of all transplants. It is a miraculous, lifesaving surgery where a perfect marriage of medicine and humanity occurs. It is the treatment of last resort for those suffering from many deadly liver diseases.

All transplants are almost surreal events. An organ is surgically retrieved from a donor, stops working, is placed on ice, travels to a recipient hospital, removed from the ice and surgically placed into the body of another person. Then the miracle happens; the organ starts working again.

There are three options for liver transplantation, cadaver donor transplantation, living donor transplantation and auxiliary transplantation.

A cadaver organ is obtained from a person who is diagnosed as brain dead whose family volunteers to donate the organ for transplant. People who receive cadaver donor organs wait on the national computer list administered by United Network of Organs Sharing (UNOS) until a suitable donor becomes available. Waiting times vary.

A living donor is a healthy family member, usually a parent, sibling, child or someone emotionally close to the patient, such as a spouse, who volunteers to donate part of their liver for transplantation. The donor is carefully evaluated to make sure no harm will come to the donor or recipient.

Living donor transplants can be done for those needing other organs as well. Other organs that may be donated by living donors are kidney, pancreas, lung and small intestine.

An auxiliary transplant is when a part of the liver of a healthy adult donor (living or cadaver) is transplanted into a recipient. The patient's diseased liver remains in tact until the auxiliary piece regenerates itself and assumes function. The diseased liver may then be removed.

Cadaver donors must meet three criteria: be brain dead, on a ventilator and in a hospital. For that reason there are five ways donors become donors; trauma, by being in an accident; gunshot wounds, usually to the head; falls; some strokes or aneurysms; and oxygen deprivation such as drowning where CPR is done, some asthma victims and some drug overdoses.

Physicians prefer matches that are made within ethnic groups to ensure the tissue is as similar to the recipient's as possible. Matches may be made and do save lives with other ethic groups, but ideally, the match is a donor of the same ethnic group. For that reason, it is important that donor awareness is sustained through racial connections and groups. There are at least two minority education groups available. Ways to contact them and others are located in the back of this book.

If you are a member of any group that would like to have a speaker come and speak about transplantation, contact your local organ procurement agency. You can find out what the name of your local organization is called by calling United Network for Organ Sharing (UNOS) in the back of this book.

Children's organ donations have dropped off largely due to the use of seat belts in cars. That is good. But, donors of young adult and middle-aged males have picked up in Texas, and in other states as well, because of the relaxed helmet law for four-wheelers and motorcycles. When I see someone riding a motorcycle without a helmet I think donor cycle. Still, as severe as the shortage of donors is, the idea is to save lives not to get donors through negligence. Wear your helmet! Fasten your seatbelt!

One donor can benefit many people. Solid organs and tissue that may be transplanted include kidneys, corneas, heart, lungs, liver, pancreas, heart valves, bone, intestine, bone marrow, skin, cartilage, ligaments and tendons.

Persons suffering cardiac death may be tissue donors but not solid organ donors. The solid organs are: heart, liver, lungs, kidneys and pancreas. A person who is pronounced cardiac dead can help people who need corneas, bone, tendons, heart valves, intestine, bone marrow, skin, cartilage ligaments and tendons.

Donors pronounced brain dead may donate the lifesaving solid organs as well as tissue.

A donor family may specify any organ or tissue they don't want to donate.

Some organs and tissue are lifesaving, some are life enhancing and some are both life saving and life enhancing. Heart, liver, kidneys, pancreas, lungs, skin and small intestine are lifesaving donations.

Anyone, regardless of age, race or gender can become an organ and tissue donor. Organs and tissue that cannot be used for transplants can be used for helping scientists find cures for serious illnesses. There is a way you may donate, whatever your cause of death.

Corneas restore vision to the blind. Skin is life saving for severely burned children and adults. Tendons are utilized to restore mobility in patients who have damaged tendons and joint injuries. Veins are utilized in vascular reconstruction to restore blood flow to various parts of the body. A person who becomes a donor with a heart that is medically unsuitable may have veins that may be used to restore blood flow for a recipient. Cartilage is connective tissue and is used for facial and other reconstructive surgery. Bone is used for correction of birth defects, facial reconstruction, limb salvage, cancer treatments, and spinal and oral surgery. Bone marrow is used for lifesaving treatment for patients with immune-deficiencies.

A donor who has a medically transplantable liver, heart, kidneys and lungs but not a transplantable pancreas, or other organ that is damaged can donate the organs that are transplantable.

Donation is not considered until all possible lifesaving efforts have failed and death has been declared. The transplant team is not notified until physicians, who have nothing to do with the transplant process, have declared death.

Donor families are not charged for donation and there is no more funeral and burial expense involved because a person donates. A traditional, open casket funeral is still possible. Organs are recovered in a careful surgical procedure.

Religious leaders the world over favor organ donation as the highest form of humanitarian ideal and consider it an act of charity.

Transplantation ethics and laws do not allow for the sale of human organs in the United States. There are those who operate tissue banks, not organ banks, for profit. It is for that reason that Southwest Transplant Alliance, the organ and tissue procurement agency in the area where I live, also operates a tissue bank, providing tissue to those in need not by selling tissue.

Age is not a factor for organ donation. To date the oldest transplanted liver is from a man eighty years old.

The organs of a deceased loved one are no longer used thus are no longer needed. We recycle so many other things that we no longer use; glass, cans, metal, tires even newspapers; why not recycle life that is so much more precious?

There are approximately 86,000 people on organ waiting lists across the country. There are 22,000 people who become brain dead annually in the U.S. There is a much greater chance that you or a loved one will need a transplant than be a donor. You or your loved one are almost four times as likely to be on a waiting list waiting for a lifesaving organ that may not come as you are to die a brain death. If you get on a transplant waiting list you are equally as likely to die waiting as you are to become a donor by brain death; very near the same amount of people who die by brain death, and donate, each year as die while waiting for a transplant that did not get there in time. An organ donor saves many lives.

...God worked unusual miracles...
Acts 19:11

26. Linda Miles

A person who has already had a transplant is a wealth of information and comfort to a waiting patient. For me that help was Ruth Ann Jones, and I was eager to help someone the way Ruth Ann had helped me.

In early April 2001, my friend Mary, who worked at a credit union office that serves several companies in our area, assisted someone who asked her how I was doing. As they discussed my recovery, the person asked Mary, "What kind of transplant did she get? I have forgotten." Mary replied, "Liver."

After the woman left, a man standing in line stepped up and asked Mary if she knew someone who had received a liver transplant. She told him about me. During their conversation, the man said that his wife was a liver disease patient and was hoping to get on the transplant waiting list. Later that day Mary called me and said she had given my phone number to the man and that his wife was very ill with liver disease. The man was Charles Miles.

I expected to hear from Charles' wife, Linda, soon since I had been so eager to talk to anyone who had already had a transplant when I first learned I had liver disease. When I didn't hear from her in a couple of weeks, I decided she might be too ill. Mary continued to see Charles at the credit union office and got reports concerning Linda's health. She was hospitalized off and on during the next few weeks. After hearing from Mary that Linda was home, and realizing from experience that Linda might not physically feel like calling me, I called her on May 17th.

Our meeting was much like the hardship times in a marriage; the toughest times are the times you are closest. We had the common experience of the hardship of a severe, life threatening disease, hepatitis C, that had progressed to end-stage liver disease for Linda.

After I told Linda who I was, I asked her if she was physically up to going out for lunch. She said she was, but I knew from the quiet sound of her weak voice how she felt. I had been there, and I also knew she was struggling to keep going. She knew to stop going meant that she might not be able to go at all. I picked her up at her house, which is not far from mine, and we went to Chili's for lunch. Linda hardly ate at all, and I understood because of my days of picking at food and having to make myself eat. On the other hand, I was still on steroids and ate as though it might have been my last meal.

When I met Linda, I was still in an almost euphoric post-transplant state. But, she was very sick; her breathing was labored and heavy, and she was uncomfortable with ascites big on her belly. She was listless and hardly moved, and when she did, she moved slowly. When one is in end-stage liver disease, even moving your hands is hard to do. Clicking the TV remote is a chore. Her speech was soft, and she was hard to hear from weakness caused by her illness.

On the way to the restaurant, I told her that since I received a new liver I felt better than I had felt in at least fifteen years. At the restaurant, we did the general get-to-know-you talk about our families. Then we talked briefly about the transplant pre-evaluation week that was coming up for her.

When we got back to her house, I showed Linda my Mercedes scar and explained about the days immediately after surgery. I told her that those days, as tough as they were, were even better than how she felt right then. We delved into the pre-transplant evaluation week, and I explained the grueling week of testing to her.

I told her thirteen weeks passed from the time of my pre-evaluation week of tests and when I got my new liver. I, like she, had waited far too long to be referred. A thirteen-week wait was extremely short; I had expected to wait at least fifteen months. I also told her I knew I would not have made a wait of fifteen months.

We talked about how frustrating the wait is, knowing that you may die waiting. Knowing that you are unable to do anything to save yourself or even to help yourself. Even more frustrating is the fact that no one else can save you or help you. I explained to her that I got to the point that if I died there was nothing I could do about it, and if I died, it was all right. I told her I didn't always know what "all right" was going to be, but I was at peace no matter what it turned out to be. And, I told her that I wasn't scared. She was very sick and was already at that point; she said she wasn't scared either. We cried. We prayed.

We discussed the pain liver disease caused our husbands. And, we cried again.

Linda's house was immaculate, but she felt otherwise and asked me if I got so I couldn't keep house. I had. I told her as she got worse physically she would have to let it go. She said she couldn't, and I understood. Leaving your house to less than your specifications is one of the hardest parts of a chronic illness. I told her after her transplant she would feel like Mr. Clean himself and with the antirejection drugs; she might even grow thick white eyebrows and muscles like his. We laughed.

We talked about her age of forty-seven being the prime of her life. She and Charles had their daughter grown and their son almost there. She had a toddler granddaughter and feared she would not live to see the little girl grow up. She wanted to make the most of her time with her family, but she felt too bad to do the things she wanted to do to make the best of that time. Tears welled up inside me at the thought of her having to leave a husband, a son, a daughter and a granddaughter, of whom I had none.

We talked about starting a support group after her surgery for those in our area who had received or needed a transplant.

In the coming weeks, we kept in touch by telephone and drop-by visits when Linda wasn't hospitalized. When she had questions, I gladly answered them. If she got scared and called, I talked to her. She didn't say she was scared, but I knew the bravado it took when she asked me about having a bleed, which I had not done, but I had experienced the same great fear of it during the wait.

In late July, Linda went for the pre-transplant evaluation, accompanied by her husband, Charles. Afterwards she became gravely ill and was transferred from the hospital in Paris to Baylor University Medical Center in Dallas, where she had been several times before.

When I went to Baylor for my one-year post-transplant checkup, Linda was already a patient there and had been in ICU for a few weeks. She was diabetic and had gotten physically worse and had been moved up to the hope of priority status 1, hospitalized and in critical need of a liver. Even though she was seriously ill, I was excited because she was as close as she could get to getting a new liver.

Later, when she was moved from ICU to a room, one of her kidneys began to fail, and she was put back in ICU. When she got out of ICU, she and I were on 14 Roberts at the same time; during my check up, the biopsy showed I was rejecting, so I was admitted. I was confined to the bed by IV medications a few times during the day and night, but otherwise, I could roam the halls, visiting or trying to walk off steroid mania, which is impossible. But, Linda was too weak and was unable to get out of bed. I visited with her and let Charles take breaks or walks. On one of his breaks when I was staying with her, in a low, weak voice she asked again what she had asked me before, "Did you get this sick?" I had to tell her no I didn't, but I knew people who had. With my friend so very sick and the emotional roller coaster caused by steroids to treat my rejection, I left Linda's room crying every time.

Her pancreas became enflamed; back to ICU once again. Then a kidney failed and she was put on dialysis. When I visited her in ICU, she asked me once again if I had gotten that sick and drifted off before I answered. It seemed whatever could go wrong with Linda did.

She was removed from the waiting list for a liver because she was too sick to undergo transplant surgery if a liver came available for her.

The last time I visited her in ICU she said, "Barb" and barely motioned with her forefinger for me to come closer. I took her hand in mine, and leaned down closer to her so I could hear her faint voice, and she whispered, "I love you." I said, "I love you too... and it's going to be all right." She already knew but at that moment we both knew what *all right* meant.

She lingered through much suffering and died on October 25, 2001, in the thirteenth week after her pre-evaluation.

Linda's thirteenth week was very different from mine. Death happens all too often in the world of transplant. Linda did not die because of lack of insurance; she and I had the same very adequate insurance. She did not die because of the lack of medical knowledge; she was at Baylor where there are world-class doctors and the liver transplant program is the best in the US. Linda died because of the lack of donors.

Her funeral was lovely. So many people were there that many had to stand outside. But, it didn't have to happen. It did not have to happen that she did not get to see her granddaughter grow up or that her granddaughter will not have her Gran Gran in her life. It did not have to happen that she didn't see her daughter, Kimberly, finish nursing school and get pinned as an RN on May 9, 2002, only six-and-a-half months after her mother's death. It did not have to happen that she never saw her son walk the road the rest of the way to manhood. It didn't have to happen that her husband can no longer hold her in his arms. It did not have to happen that her mother saw one of her children buried.

Linda's story could be your story or that of one of your loved ones. Sixteen people die everyday in the US while waiting for a transplant.

I knew Linda only a bit over five months, but I felt like I had known her for years as we laughed and cried together. We were much more unlike than alike. I had no children and no grandchildren; she had both. I had enjoyed working out of the home all my life; she was domestic and lived her life for her family and loved it. Our closeness was the bond of sharing hardship.

I am glad to have known her, briefly though it was, and to have shared the hardship of her illness and the hope of transplant with her. I would have loved to be able to start the support group for liver transplant patients in our area with her in it as we talked about doing after she received her transplant.

When we met, Linda was walking in the boots I had worn for so long, but when it ended she had walked in my boots, but I did not walk in hers. For that I am grateful, and wish I could be saying that for Linda too.

When Linda died I thought I could not do again what Ruth Ann had done for me. It was too painful... but I can and I will.

Linda

God came for an angel
He could not wait for
He wrapped her in his arms
And carried her safely home.

To a place without suffering and tears
A place without months and years
If we could see her now in the sky
We would not cry.

She was not afraid to go
Down that path she did not know
God is caring for her now
She is an angel we know.

Barba Covington McCarty
October 25, 2001

27. Others Who Have Stood in My Boots

... there is but a step between me and death.
I Samuel 20:3

T hough it may not seem like it, there are others who have stood in our boots at different places and different times. My story is specifically mine. For informational reasons, I offer other stories of friends I have met and shared experiences with along my journey.

To people who are uninformed, liver disease may mean that the sufferer deserves his or her liver disease and the fate that goes with it because they made lifestyle choices by abusing alcohol or drugs or getting a tattoo or having many sex partners, and all of these actions may indeed be the cause of irreversible liver damage for many. However, bad lifestyle choices are not the only reasons for liver transplant, but even if they were, will the person who has lived his or her life without making a bad choice, please stand up?

I must admit, when I first found out about my liver disease, these thoughts entered my mind because I had been so extra careful to do the things that were right for my body. Often my thoughts and understanding concerning people who had made bad lifestyle choices in their lives and were paying for it was selective at best. Some of them were in the transplant waiting lineup, and some, I knew, were ahead of those who had not made the poor lifestyle choices. Later, I succumbed to the fact that people change, and those changes must take place before one can get a liver transplant. There is a six-month sobriety requirement from drugs or alcohol before anyone is eligible for a liver transplant; if lab tests show alcohol or drugs at any time while waiting, the patient becomes ineligible and is removed from the waiting list.

I still get very angry when I hear of those who return to their old habits, their lifesaving transplanted liver fails, and they return for another transplant. They take three livers—lives—with them when they go; the one they had to begin with, the one they received so freely from a donor family and the one who died that would have received the organ that he or she wasted.

I am aware of one who has already received two organs and is in need of a third because of drinking alcohol. He proved himself by abstaining from alcohol for the required six months each of the two times he was transplanted. He is not the norm of those who get liver transplants due to alcoholic cirrhosis; he is the extraordinary exception. It is my understanding that he has decided not to go for a third transplant, and instead, is still drinking alcohol. In his case, there were six wasted livers; the three listed above, a second donor liver he suffocated in a lake of alcohol and another person who died waiting for the second liver he drowned, and eventually, he will go. This is an offence I cannot tolerate; there are not enough organs. For someone to waste precious donated organs, abhors me and, on this matter, I am unforgiving.

In the last few decades, there have been more than one hundred causes, other than alcohol and drug abuse, that have been recognized by the medical community as causes of liver diseases and damage, some of them as innocent as taking over-the-counter medications.

I tell you about others who have walked in my boots to let you know some of the other reasons for liver transplant and other complications of liver disease.

Ruth Ann Jones, My Liver Buddy, Hepatitis C (HCV)

Ruth Ann shared much more than information with me; she also shared her story for this book.

As far as Ruth Ann knows, she contracted HCV from her husband of just over five years; even though it is rare that hepatitis C is caught through sexual contact, when it does happen, it's more common for a female to contract the disease from a male than for males to contract it from females. And, she may have contracted the disease by means other than sexual contact from him; she could have had an open wound that he bled on, used his nail clippers with a minute amount of his blood on them, or a razor, toothbrush or nail file. With this disease most do not know how they contracted it.

Ruth had no symptoms and was indeed not at the lab for any symptoms of liver disease when she was diagnosed, as so many with HCV are. She went in for surgery on her wrist and blood tests came back irregular.

The orthopedic doctor who removed a ganglion cyst from her wrist referred her to a hematology clinic, for follow up on the irregular blood tests. At the hematology clinic she underwent many tests, among them a bone marrow test because it was thought she might have leukemia. Her test for leukemia proved negative, and she was then referred to a gastroenterologist. As she waited the three-and-a-half months to work through all the different doctors, clinics and test results, she was not too much concerned because the leukemia test was negative, and she was reasonably sure it wasn't anything serious. She thought possibly she was just anemic until early 1990 when a biopsy revealed her liver was already severely damaged.

Her husband was unaware he was infected with HCV until after Ruth was diagnosed and he was tested. In 1980, he was given a transfusion after surgery for bleeding ulcers, and as far as he knows, that is when he was infected.

Ruth became too ill to continue working as a cosmetologist in February 1994. Her complication was her pulmonary function; she had varices in her lungs that caused her not to get enough oxygen. She had to have oxygen part time for a year and advanced to "oxygen on a rope," that, for Ruth Ann, was indeed life on a rope, full time for a full six months before her transplant on July 1, 1997. She was on the list ten months when she got her transplant.

Ruth's donor was a thirty-year-old female who Ruth thinks of often. She has not heard from her donor family after writing a thank you letter to them, but says she thinks often of writing them again to let them know she is still doing well. She says she is afraid if she met her donor's family that all she could do is cry.

And, Ruth Ann says she has thought much and often about another woman, the woman who had to be removed from the transplant waiting list because she, like my friend Linda, became too ill to go through the surgery and died afterwards. Ruth feels she got the liver that woman would have gotten had she been able to withstand the surgery of transplant. And, she is probably right. In the world of transplant it is most likely we all got an organ that someone else would have gotten had they not gotten too ill to withstand the surgery and died as a result of that. It is a fact of life—and death—in the transplant world.

When I asked her if she would do it again, she smiled softly, as she does, and answered quietly, "yes." But, when I asked her to describe her life now, she exclaimed in a loud one-word answer, "Wonderful." She says after so long, she is now back to her normal self since her transplant. She cannot do everything she once could, but she can do so much more than she could before. She works in her garden, and goes RVing with her husband for weeks at a time. She quilts and sews and enjoys her grandchildren and cares for her mother more since her father died last year.

Before her transplant, Ruth could barely take a shower by herself, and her husband had to wash her hair for her because she was too weak to hold her hands over her head to do it alone. Her husband worked and then came home to cook and clean and do all the chores she had done before she got too ill, while she sat in a chair and cried because he was doing what she could no longer do. Ruth says without her husband and family, her road to transplant would have been much harder, and she appreciates them greatly.

As wonderful as her life is now, when she went back for her five-year checkup in July 2001, she was diagnosed diabetic; antirejection medication that she must take is the believed cause of the diabetes. She finds it hard to eat three meals and three snacks per day and to give her injections twice daily with insulin along with her antirejection medication regime required after transplant.

Ruth Ann says she was bitter about the fact that she caught the disease from her husband for a long time but has long since gotten over the bitterness.

Her husband still has the disease. He has had it much longer than she has but he has not gotten ill enough to require a transplant.

As far as she knows, she had HCV only thirteen years before she was in end-stage liver disease and needed a transplant. Her husband may have had the disease already for twenty-two years and still has not reached that stage, but he has fatigue much more frequently now.

Today, as we talked for this writing while sitting on stools at Burger Land having old fashioned hamburgers, and I told her of Jerri's, another transplant friend's, dilemma of possibly getting a kidney transplant after having gone through a liver transplant she said she's not sure she would do that. When I questioned her further, because she had already told me if she had to do a liver transplant again she would, she said, "I'm already to the point of if they run out of pills and parts I'm in trouble." We laughed. I said to her, "I thought possibly you thought it might get a little crowded in there." Then she said, "I might not know who was me." We enjoyed our visit.

When I was hospitalized for my transplant and Ruth Ann came to visit me, appropriately, she brought an angel she had embroidered. It sits on my mantle today.

Jerri Major, Primary Schlerosing Cholangitis (PSC)

Jerri Major, the mother-in-law of ICU nurse Sayda Major who I spoke of in chapter 20 received the donated liver of a thirty-five year old female in November 1999 at the age of sixty-six, after years of illnesses and surgeries. In 1983 Jerri had unbearable severe itching that first took her to the doctor when she was diagnosed with ulcerative colitis. She had experienced constipation a long time before and had been given medication, so when she began to have less and less problems with constipation she thought she was finally "normal." Her new normalcy was not normal, and later, her problems with ulcerative colitis resulted in an iliostomy, a surgical incision creating an artificial opening in the lower part of the small intestine. Near the time she had the iliostomy, she was diagnosed with Primary Schlerosing Cholangitis, PSC, a degenerative disease that enflames and scars bile ducts, causing them to progressively decrease in size. As a result, bile that is normally carried out of the liver accumulates within the liver, which then damages the liver cells and causes the liver to fail. The exact cause of PSC is unknown. It affects more men than women and may occur alone but is often associated with inflammatory diseases of the colon like ulcerative colitis. Many people have no symptoms for years.

During the next sixteen years, after Jerri was diagnosed with ulcerative colitis and had the iliostomy, she was hospitalized numerous times because of bleeds from the veins at the site of the iliostomy.

As PSC progressed, she grew more fatigued, jaundiced and had fevers and chills. Her health deteriorated to the point of her needing a liver transplant that she received in 2000.

Now, Jerri has an enjoyable life and stays busy. She does indeed stay busy. She goes to church, walks one-and-a-half miles daily, is in a quilting group, acts as secretary-treasurer of a cemetery association, loves to garden and with her husband of fifty-one years, is considering building a house. The day after my interview with her, she had plans to help cook and serve lunch to the seniors at a nearby high school.

When I asked Paul Major, Jerri's husband, if she was different since the transplant, he said, "When she first woke up in ICU her eyes were brighter and her color was better. She got out of the hospital on her fifth day after transplant and started walking, and she has never quit."

But, with all Jerri does, she is having problems. Her kidneys are failing, caused by the antirejection medications she takes for her liver graft, and the doctors are talking kidney transplant now. She is lightly jaundiced and the tops of her arms and hands to her elbows are black and blue, not in circles like bumps and bruises, totally dark-blue-on-the-way-to-black from her elbows to her fingers. The doctors tell her that the discoloration is caused by the antirejection therapy.

She smiled and said, "I look a mess, but I feel good. I consider myself lucky. I dread another transplant and might not do it, but the children insist that I do." Kevin, her youngest, who is married to the ICU nurse Sayda, has even offered her one of his kidneys, but she has not decided to take it yet.

She said she would do it all again, knowing what she knows now. When she was first diagnosed, Kevin, her youngest child of four children was only twelve years old and she would have missed seeing him grow up, she said.

Wanda Hughes, Unknown Kidney Disease

Wanda Hughes began having kidney problems during her pregnancy in 1965. After the delivery of her son, she continued to suffer frequent kidney infections for a reason that could not be determined.

Years later, in 1983, kidney infections with burning symptoms was not the reason she went to her doctor. She had begun having severe pain in her arms and legs and was sent to a neurologist who determined that the pain was caused by fluid build-up in her body.

A few weeks later, her blood pressure got extremely high, and medication did not work to lower it. Further tests discovered that her kidneys had failed. On March 16, 1983, she was diagnosed with end-stage renal failure.

Wanda's health was so bad that she could no longer walk. Her son was now eighteen years old. Wanda recalls telling the nurses on the day of her diagnosed kidney failure, "You've got to keep me alive until my son graduates." In April of that year, she was put on dialysis three times a week for four hours each time and did see her son graduate, but she had no idea what all was in store for her afterwards.

She worked at the Coca Cola Company in Paris, Texas, but because of dialysis, she was available to work only two days of the week. The company asked her to retire at the age of thirty-nine, because they needed to have a full-time employee. She was so sick the two days each week she worked that she could hardly get there, so she agreed to their proposal and quit working

Her problems continued, and she was put on the list for a kidney transplant in Oklahoma City. She received a long-awaited kidney from a thirty-year-old female from Oklahoma City on September 23, 1986. But, her new kidney only worked six days; a blood clot formed in the new kidney and caused it to fail. It was back to dialysis for Wanda. Her new kidney that failed could have stayed in place until she got another transplant but three weeks after her new kidney failed, complications arose, and she had to be ambulanced back to Oklahoma City to get the kidney removed. After surgery, she came home again and was back on dialysis for four more years.

After the experience of a seven-and-a-half-hour surgery for a kidney that only lasted six days and an additional surgery to remove the failed kidney she vowed not to have another transplant and told her husband, "I am going to die on dialysis." She stayed in that state of mind for a full two years when she saw her gynecologist in Paris, Texas, Dr. Robert Yeakley, and told him that she had decided not to undergo another transplant that she had decided she was going to live as long as dialysis worked and would die on dialysis. During this visit Dr, Yeakley took a lot of extra time with her. He told her that she was so young and that he believed if she tried again she could have a good life. She gave it thought for the first time since her transplanted kidney failed and she had to have it removed, and the next day at dialysis, she told the woman who worked with transplant patients, "I have decided I want to go back and get on the list for a kidney. This time I want to go to Dallas, though." She chose not to go back to the same place where he first kidney failed for another transplant.

Her renal doctor referred her to the Methodist hospital in Dallas, and her local dialysis center made the arrangements. After extensive testing six weeks later, she was on the list for another kidney. She waited about two more years before her perfect-match kidney became available. The doctors at Methodist hospital in Dallas told her the only way a kidney could have been a better match was if she had received the kidney from her twin but Wanda did not have a twin.

Her perfectly matched kidney came from a thirty-five year old male from San Diego, California, and was flown to Texas for her surgery on April 14, 1990. Her second transplant has gone well, with no signs of rejection or complications.

On the first year anniversary of her new kidney, her husband came in carrying flowers and said he couldn't let this day pass without it. So, every year on the anniversary of her transplant, she and her husband do something in her donors' honor; they buy flowers and have a prayer. This year they planted an azalea in their yard in honor of her donors.

When Wanda talks about Dr. Yeakley and the conversation in his office that changed her mind about getting a second transplant, she gets very emotional. When I asked her if she would do it all again, her reply was, "I'm so glad I had the second transplant."

Wanda has dark spots on her arms and hands from taking steroids for twelve years, but she has such fear of rejecting her precious perfectly matched kidney that she prefers to stay on the steroids, instead of being taken off them. When the doctors wanted to reduce her steroids, she declined. She has no other effects from the steroids and is adamant about staying on them.

She goes one hundred miles to Dallas every three months for her lab work, and at her last checkup she was doing great. In her new life now, she enjoys her fourteen-year-old granddaughter; she and her husband enjoy fishing together and traveling; and she enjoys cooking and working in her yard, two tasks she had given up because of her ill health before.

Dr. Yeakley was right. Wanda is having a good life. She would have missed so much had she not gone for another transplant. She calls it "another gift of life."

One of the things she would have missed would have been seeing her granddaughter that she loves so much, grow up.

My Nephew, Dan, Hepatitis C

On September 19, 2000, eighteen days before I received my lifesaving liver transplant, my nephew Dan worked on his friend Dorlas' pickup truck then drove her to the hospital to get X-rays on a shoulder injury she had sustained. As they sat waiting for Dorlas' turn at X-ray, Dan became nauseated and excused himself to the men's room where he vomited a large amount of blood. He returned to the waiting room and told Dorlas about it just as she was called to get her X-rays. Dorlas summoned an X-ray technician who volunteered to walk Dan across the hall to the ER while she was X-rayed. Twenty minutes later, when Dorlas went to the ER to check on Dan, he was already in ICU.

Dan had advanced cirrhosis and hepatitis C and had experienced a variceal bleed, and until he vomited the vast amount of blood, he had no idea he was sick.

He had experienced frequent nosebleeds, which he and Dorlas thought might be caused from high blood pressure, but he had checked his blood pressure at home, and it was not elevated. He did have a few scattered spider veins across his chest but did not know what they were; they didn't hurt so he wasn't worried about them. He had drunk a lot of alcohol, in earlier years but had cut down considerably. Now he only drank beer, which is still alcohol. He had received a blood transfusion in 1983 when he sustained a leg laceration while doing construction work.

He did not have fevers, night sweats or weight loss. He had full-mouth teeth extraction earlier in September and had no excessive bleeding. He did not have ascites or jaundice. He had not been to a doctor, because until the day he had vomited blood, he felt fine.

He went home from the hospital and drank no more beer, a cold turkey quit with Dorlas' help, to save his life.

Dan's was a case where HCV was silent until his liver was gone. He lived his last months with the knowledge that he had assisted in its demise by drinking alcohol for many years.

In March, when I had recovered from my transplant enough to travel alone and after he had quit all alcohol and was about to begin interferon therapy, Dorlas and Dan had a family gathering at their home. There I had possibly the only three minutes alone with him since his illness was discovered. As we sat in his backyard, talking about his illness and before others interrupted us, he told me, "I had a good life, Barb. I had a lot of fun..."

Barba Covington McCarty

He laughed a half laugh, and after a long pause, he added, "killing myself" and grinned like he did.

In April, when he was beer free for six months, he and Dorlas attended patient education on HCV and pegylated interferon treatment. Dorlas administered his medicine weekly for six months. Later, he began to have lung complications and was hospitalized. He had "life (oxygen) on a rope" connected to him all the time.

As with most patients taking treatment for hepatitis, more than one round is necessary. He started a second six-month session in November and was able to take it only four weeks because of his rapidly declining pulmonary health.

His care, even when he did get care so late in his disease, was mismanaged. In medical reports I have before me, the gastroenterologist who treated him when he was first hospitalized for the bleed stated that transplant was "out of the question because he would have to be off alcohol for over two years to be considered."

In March Dan's younger brother drove seven hours for a visit to offer him part of his liver in a living donor transplant, but Dan was under the impression from his gastroenterologist that he had to have two full years of sobriety. This is not true; Baylor's requirement is six months of sobriety. When his brother came and made the offer of part of his liver to him he was at six-months of sobriety and would have met the requirement.

Had his gastroenterologist given Dan correct information, he would have been eligible to get evaluated for transplant in March 2001. In the ten months he lived after that requirement was met he became very ill and was hospitalized in ICU for complications. At that time, he might have been moved up on the transplant waiting list to priority status 1 and might have received a transplant that would have saved his life. Or perhaps his brother, who so compassionately volunteered part of his liver to Dan, would have been a compatible match, and he might not have had to wait on the list at all. He possibly could have had half of his brother's liver in March after he completed six months of sobriety after the bleed occurred. Dan might be alive today had the correct information been conveyed to him.

Being from a family that knows about lifesaving transplants, because I had just received my liver in October 2000, Dan had decided to donate his organs that—according to medical reports before me—were all in good working order except his liver and lungs. When near the end, Dorlas mentioned donation to a nurse in ICU, the nurse replied, "He can't donate his organs because he has hepatitis." Dorlas, knowing no better did not question the knowledge of the ICU nurse. As Dorlas as I talked about the medical reports today, she said to me, "Dan was in good shape for the shape he was in." She said that because medical reports showed his heart was strong and his pancreas and kidneys were in good condition.

Dan's organs could have been donated to patients who had HCV and were waiting on transplant waiting lists for a heart, kidney or a pancreas. For those patients with HCV a heart, kidney or pancreas will save their life without infecting them with HCV that they already have. Possibly five are dead today because of misinformation in the medical community that we trust to save our lives—Dan and four others who had hepatitis, but were waiting for an organ, who would have received his heart, kidneys and pancreas.

I reported this incident to the transplant procurement agency that does the training for nurse liaisons who initiate organ donation after a patient is pronounced brain dead in ICU (where patients are most likely to be when they become potential organ donors,) and they have initiated a more thorough teaching to the nurse liaisons.

Dan died at the age of fifty-one on January 28, 2002, of lung complications due to liver disease—just sixteen months and nine days after he was diagnosed with liver disease. In addition to his full name, date of birth, date of death and his parents names his gravestone carries the words, "Go With the Flow."

I tell you about my nephew's illness to let you know how severely ill one can get with liver disease with no idea they have an illness at all, and I tell you to let you know that those in the medical field are only human; they make mistakes or may not have the correct information that might save lives. You cannot have too much information to use in your quest for your own health.

I remember very little of Dan's illness when he was first diagnosed with the variceal bleed, as I was so very ill and under the influence of encephalopathy. I had received my transplant only eighteen days after his variceal bleed incident occurred. As he grew physically worse, when the misinformation incident with the ICU nurse occurred, I had been hospitalized for rejection and had had several complications from the treatment of the rejection that kept me from traveling the sixty miles to see him or from knowing as much as I would have normally known about his condition.

Unlike Linda Miles, Dan did not have a daughter, a son and granddaughter, but he had Dorlas who misses him greatly, a mother who lost her first-born son, a brother who cared enough to put his own life in jeopardy to save Dan's, a sister, a niece and nephew and three great-nephews and several aunts, all who loved him and miss him.

Barba Covington McCarty

28. I Made It!

Now, I know for certain that the Lord has sent His angel and rescued me...
Acts 12:11

I returned home almost four months after Sherri and I left early on the rainy morning of October 6, 2000. I cried when my sister, Betty, turned the corner to the street where I live and I could see my pink brick house waiting for my return to the rhythm of life. I had made it to day one of the rest of my life, and it was a new life. Even though I was still a bit weak, I arrived in far better health than when I left almost four months before, and when asked how I felt, I said I felt better than I had in at least fifteen years. I was still a little scared because I had left the watchful eyes of those at the hospital, and the responsibility fell on me to notice any symptoms of rejection or infection.

I weighed in at 132 pounds when I returned home. I still did not have the appetite everyone else had at Twice Blessed House, even without the "grassy" (herbed) hospital foods that I hated. I shrugged it off as maybe it was an effect of the stroke I had. I bought new "little" clothes and loved it. About the time I got a drawer full of new size 6 panties and 34 C bras—just when I was considering getting a thong—near the end of February, my appetite uninvited and unexpectedly arrived. I got out the food pyramid that I had been given in nutrition class and began my new life of eating healthy as directed. I tried hard everyday to eat six servings in the bread group, three in the vegetable group, two in the fruit group and two in the meat group. I kept a log of everything I ate, and at days end, I graded myself on how I did on the pyramid. I never got an A, the grade I would have gotten had I been able to eat all of the servings I was supposed to. I was not one to snack between meals, but in an effort to build and eat a pyramid, I added snacks. Still, I could not eat a pyramid, but I kept at it, and somewhere along the way, I discovered all the tasty foods I had missed for so long. Soon, I was ignoring the pyramid and eating everything. I have experienced a weight problem most of my adult life. But still, being a chubette—that's English for fat—I had never once gone to the refrigerator in the middle of the night. But, now I did. If I saw something advertised on TV, I went to the store, or wherever, and got it. Once, after seeing an ad on TV I went out in the rain, in my clean car, at eleven o'clock at night to go to Wal-Mart to get a Butterfinger—me, who will avoid trips in the rain to keep my car clean. I cooked the things I had not had, nor wanted, for so many years. One night at ten-thirty, I made chicken spaghetti that I had never once made or tried to make before. I feared that, if offered, I might eat a pickled egg or a pig's foot. Along with that non-stop party in my mouth I was having came a drawer full of new size 7 panties, then size 8, then size 9 and... finally, I stopped with enough panties to stock a good sized store. With one more reduction in dosage, I am hoping to be off steroids really soon.

I have come to realize that steroids and weight gain have something in common with cold weather and rain and the flu; cold weather or rain does not give you a cold or the flu, germs do, and steroids do not cause you to gain weight, eating does. But it's hard to have one without the other.

At any rate, weight began to pile on with my steroid-enhanced taste buds, so to get control of it, I went to Baylor for my yearly checkup a day early to meet with a dietician Jeanette, at Baylor; who had tried so hard to get me to eat anything while I was hospitalized and was now counseling me about eating too much. Before I made the appointment with her, I knew that I knew what to do and how to do it, but I still needed the problem addressed. It is required that anyone getting a transplant attend four outpatient nutrition classes taught by transplant dieticians before being dismissed. I attended those four classes along with everyone else, only a lot of the time I was thinking "I don't do that anyway" because for years before my transplant, I didn't. I did not eat fried foods, potato chips, and butter on anything but a steak from the local Fish Fry Restaurant, candy, sweets and foods that were not good for me. I would not have eaten a frankfurter, corn dog, Spam, deviled ham, or potted meat for anything for years, not because I did not like them, but because they were high in fat and cholesterol. And, even though I didn't like those things, even though I had never had problems with cholesterol, I didn't eat them to prevent having any problems with cholesterol. For the years closest to my transplant time, I had to make myself eat, even the things I once liked.

When I was waiting to meet with the dietician, I saw Dr. Levy and told him I was concerned about my weight gain, fifty pounds in seven months. He said, "I can see you have tried everything, and you liked it." He was right; for a few weeks, I ate Sonic cheese coneys at least three times a week and had even tried potted meat and deviled ham (thank goodness I still didn't like them).

Now, after meeting with Jeanette, the dietician, the problem has only slightly improved; or I should say, I have only slightly improved the problem. I no longer go to the refrigerator in the middle of the night or out in the rain to Wal-Mart for Butterfingers, and I no longer cook chicken spaghetti at ten-thirty at night, but I wouldn't win a ribbon, or even place in the nutrition game. My weight is still a big problem.

* * *

I'm back; I am at the first proof read of this book and had just read about eating Sonic cheese coneys near suppertime. Although, I have not had a cheese coney in months, I left the computer, got in my Buick and drove in the rain right down to the Sonic and had one, minus the mustard, which is the only thing on a cheese coney that might be all right for me to eat. At least I didn't go to Wal-Mart and get a Butterfinger too.

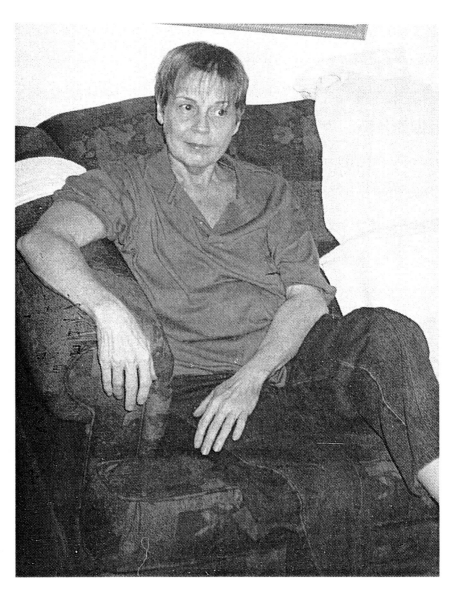

I Made It!

When I first got home, I was possessed-like with catching up on everything I had missed. I visited friends and relatives and they visited me. I went out to eat with anyone who came by or called. I attended "Girls Night Out," a local yearly outing for women in Paris and I attended the transplant reunion at Baylor where everyone was surprised to see me. I had no idea they thought that I would not make it when I was living at Twice Blessed House, going through all the complications. I enjoyed Covington Cousin's Day, my family reunion, like I hadn't in years. And, on Friday, the 13th of April, I planted periwinkles for the first time since 1993. I even attended a Pampered Chef party and a Home Interior party and enjoyed them (I don't usually like home parties). I helped Darlyn straighten up after a move to a new house and attended Phyllis's granddaughter's gym recital. I attended meetings for planning my 35th class reunion and renewed old acquaintances. Did I mention I went to eat with anyone who called or came by? I was in an almost euphoric state where I recommended liver transplants to everyone.

At first, your life is taken away, then it is given back. I have been given the chance to go around again. That makes life much more precious. Something as minute as using your very own potty becomes special. The day I got home after having been gone so long, I felt like a toddler must feel when getting praised for using the potty. And, not being praised for it was yet another blessing... for "not making it" had happened to me once during the early transplant recovery period. The big thing now was that no one was around when I used it and it was *my* potty.

I had missed things that I didn't even realize. There were many new items in the grocery store. I know, Dr. Levy was right; I've tried them all now.

I envisioned life after transplant as a new beginning. Soon I was running around everywhere in my post-transplant, almost euphoric state, all the time feeling free and normal again. But, when I got home, my sisters envisioned me still being reachable twenty-four hours a day, as I had been for several years and that I must not be far from medical care. It took many months, before I could get them not to get in a spin if I wasn't home when they called. Months later, just as they were about through the pains of adjusting to my new life, I had a rejection. I was hospitalized and had complications from the high-dose steroids that treated the rejection. The complications affected my eyesight and lowered my blood pressure afterwards and warranted me staying home for about four months. On the first day I was out and about afterwards, my sister, Betty, called, and when I wasn't home, she called Beverly. When I didn't answer a second time, she called Beverly again. The third time Betty called her, Beverly got in on the search by calling Phyllis who was out of town on a school field trip. Then she called Fay; Fay didn't answer. April was visiting in California and didn't answer her home or cell phone numbers. She called my running buddy Ben's number and when I answered the phone because I was closest to it in the kitchen, she demanded, "Where have you been all day? We've been looking for you since early this morning."

Retraining them began again. Beverly is easy to train but there are those who are harder to train; so it is with our sister, Betty. I do understand and appreciate their concern. After all it was my illness that made me reachable at home for so many years.

I have learned that you can handle anything life throws your way, and that you have to laugh to breath.

I have learned that the gift of chronic illness and pain is the pathway to the increased sense of joy. I have learned that lemons are the sour bitter days of life that make it seem all the better later.

I have learned that there really are angels and that they aren't flying around near the ceiling in white silk gowns with wings and gold halos and that they are not on walls in pictures. They are people you don't even know and those you do know that you might never suspect led a double life moonlighting as an angel. And, I have learned that I am not tired of angels; as I thought the day Fay and I shopped so long ago.

Before my transplant, I never once, consciously thought *dying is not an option.* That was an attitude. That positive attitude is a coping mechanism that I used to stay alive until a liver became available for me. A positive attitude is a must. In reality the option to live or die did not exist for me or for anyone awaiting a transplant. That option lies with donor families; in my case it was Terry Sharp's family and I am so glad they chose the option to share life. For those still waiting, the option may be yours... or mine... or your families... or mine.

A year later, just about the time I was beginning to claim Terry's liver as my own, I suffered an acute (class A-1) rejection. I was treated for it and have done well since. Rejection can happen from now on for the rest of my life. Rejections can happen for no reason and there are things one can do that cause rejection; like not taking medications correctly. In my post-transplant world this does not happen. I am quite possibly fanatical about taking my medications. Still, rejection can happen without a cause. It is the gamble of transplant.

The symptoms of rejection vary with each patient, and the following symptoms may not always mean rejection, but you should call your coordinator if you have just one of the following symptoms. Fever—a temperature over 100 degrees; flu-like symptoms, chills, nausea, vomiting, diarrhea, headache, dizziness, body aches and pains; dark tea-colored urine; clay-colored stools; change in color of your urine to dark yellow or orange; decreased appetite; pain and or tenderness in the abdomen or in the area of your transplant scar; ascites; fatigue; excess sleepiness or lethargy; weight gain; yellowing of your eyes or skin; itching; lower than normal blood pressure or shortness of breath.

If you have only one of these symptoms call your doctor or transplant coordinator. Early detection can be a lifesaver.

After having been ill for so long I am still adjusting to my new state of health. Recently, I had a temperature and didn't realize it but after I sat watching TV for a couple of hours, which I never do, it hit me that *something's making me fall in this chair every time I pass it.* So, I took my temperature and had a fever. Before my transplant a very low-grade temperature made me feel so bad that I had to go to bed but now that I'm like everyone else I can a have a low-grade temp and not realize it. I don't notice I am ill until I am ill for awhile after all those years of being used to constantly illness. Pain, discomfort and sickness were a way of life and if you have lived that way for a long time you think pain, discomfort and sickness is normal. It's a hard chain of thought to break.

Elevated lab reports can mean a possible rejection episode, but only a liver biopsy can confirm rejection. I had no symptoms and was at the hospital for my yearly checkup when a biopsy showed I was rejecting. Do not try to diagnose yourself or treat yourself.

The symptoms of infection are: fever, headache, shortness of breath, a dry or productive cough, diarrhea and/or a burning sensation with urination. Call your doctor and get treatment started as soon as possible, as simple illnesses for someone else may mean severe illness for the immunosuppressed. Immunosuppressed people have had their immune systems turned off by the antirejection medications that we are required to take.

A person does not emerge from a transplant like a new person, free of taking medication or having health concerns. You must emerge from transplant as a team player in your own health care. As I have said before, at five months post transplant, I felt so well that I was in an almost euphoric state, and my life is changed but it not free of restrictions. Along with blood tests forever, a transplant patient adopts a whole new regime of medication demands along with side effects of those medications. I take cyclosporin, a gel cap that when opened has the faint odor of a skunk in the distance. I have cut one of the gel caps open and the gel inside does not have that odor. It was approved by the Federal Drug Administration in 1981 and revolutionized the world of liver transplant, making it no longer experimental surgery. The success rate went from 25 to 30 percent to 75 to 80 percent. Cyclosporin carries with it the side effects of increased hair growth and darkened hair color. But I, with the help of L'OREAL #9A, fixed that; I simply could not be going around with darkened hair after half a century of being very light blond. Other side effects of this medication are hand tremors, a big problem for me the first weeks. Others include nasal congestion, swollen gums, high blood pressure, high cholesterol, flushing and occasional tingling hands and an increased sex drive. I have experienced all of them except an increased sex drive. Just my luck to miss the fun one.

Everyone doesn't have all of the side effects, and they do not linger forever. Some of my side effects happened when I first began cyclosporin therapy and no longer bother me. And, as I said before, some have not gotten here yet, but I'm still waiting. The new regime, along with the side effects of it, is as much a part of my life now as liver disease was before; only I feel better. If I am allowed to cast a vote, I certainly prefer the new regime and its side effects.

My life is not totally free of the lion that ruled my life for so long. I still have hepatitis C, but, thanks to Terry and his family, I no longer have the cirhossed liver it caused. I do not live my life in an autoclave, but I have adopted a new set of rules to live by such as not going where there are large crowds of people, because immunosuppressed people get infections easily during the first year after transplant, for me that time was up in October, the beginning of cold and flu season, so I continued avoiding such places until spring. One of those places is church, which I miss, but everyone at church shakes your hand and I am a hugger, so I get lots of hugs. Also, the truly faithful will attend church when they are sick. I am coming up on summer, and plan to start back soon. It is also recommended that I avoid hospitals and nursing homes because of contagious illnesses there.

Very recently, I drove seven hours to visit one of my sisters who was hospitalized for lymphoma. I arrived at her room, walking behind another person. The door was standing open so I did not see the isolation sign on my sister's hospital room door. As we sat talking in her room nearly an hour later, my sick sister mentioned that no one could be put in the other bed in her room and that the hospital was full. I asked why they couldn't use the other bed, and she replied, "Because I'm in isolation." I froze. I didn't want to upset my already very ill sister so in a few minutes I excused myself to the nurses' station and asked why she was in isolation. She had shingles. I left the hospital and called the transplant office at BUMC to inquire, although I already knew the answer. The virus that causes shingles is the same one that causes chicken pox. Most would have to touch the open shingle lesion to catch the virus. For me, being immunosuppressed, I could possibly contract it in the air, the way chicken pox is spread. I tell you this to let those of you waiting for a transplant know that you are the one responsible for your well being after you leave the womb of the hospital setting. Even those closest to you may not remember the new rules for your life. Beverly, my little sister, had been to visit our sister the week before I went, and I talked to Beverly on the phone twice every day she was there. Even though she knows I am immunosuppressed and need not to be around anyone who is ill, she did not remember to tell me our sister was in isolation. It didn't enter her mind, as it doesn't enter her mind to tell me when one of her grandchildren is ill and I plan a visit to her house. So... I ask before I go, "Is anybody sick?"

I have fallen in the baihtub recently and sustained a rotator cuff injury. I cannot take the prescribed Ibuprofen because it is hard on my kidneys, which are already taxed by the transplant medications. For this reason, if you have a doubt or question about the medicine prescribed by another doctor, call your transplant doctor. I am allowed to take Tylenol, Immodium, Benadryl and cold medications if necessary. Do not use anything, including over-the-counter vitamins or herbal remedies before consulting with your transplant coordinator or transplant doctor.

Just yesterday I visited the office of a specialty dentist that I was referred to. He entered the room where I was waiting, carrying a tongue depressor and already wearing gloves, and that is good, but he opened the door with his gloved hand on the doorknob and had been elsewhere, possibly in another patient's room, wearing the gloves. So when he stood before me with a tongue depressor to check inside my mouth, I said, "No, I'm immunosuppressed, and you came in with those gloves on." He paused and then said, "I'm just going to look inside with this" and showed the tongue depressor to me. I said, "No, you're not. Not until you change gloves and get a new depressor" which he did, but as he put one new glove on he laid the other new glove down on the counter. We had another bout of conflict over the gloves. I am responsible and careful about my own health care, and I am not bashful about it, but I am vigilant. When I questioned him, I was not hostile, loud or accusatory. Thank goodness the problem I was sent to this dentist for was not there, because I will not see him again. I am sure his purpose for the gloved hands when he entered the exam room was for his protection, and that is good; I have HCV and it was on the front of my chart in huge red letters. He is responsible for his protection, and so am I for mine. But... I was paying monetarily for my protection, and I have no intention of paying with my life that I have fought so hard to save, because of possible infection. He was a bit taken aback by my actions and did not like it, but neither did I like his actions. Where my health and safety is concerned, I am the one that has to like it.

In another instance, I have had a lab technician come at me with her needle without gloves. I said, "I have hepatitis C; you need gloves." She said, "Ohh, I'm OK. I'm not going to stick myself." My reply to her was, "And, you're not going to stick me, either, until you put gloves on." She put gloves on every time thereafter. I do not let lab techs lay cotton down on the arm of the chair where I have bled before when I was getting a test. I am sure I am not the only patient who has ever bled on the arm of a lab chair.

I must never again receive a live or weakened virus vaccine such as smallpox, yellow fever, measles, mumps, rubella and oral polio vaccine. I do not get close to a child who has taken oral polio vaccine since there is a chance that I might contract the poliovirus. This type of vaccination gives a small dose of the actual virus, which, in turn, could turn into serious complications for me. Only diphtheria-tetanus (boosters only) are allowed and vaccines for the flu, mantoux (TB) and the pneumococcal vaccines. I have heard reports on TV about the possibility of smallpox vaccinations starting up again in the US in the fight against terrorism, and I wonder—what happens to those of us who are immunosuppressed? We will not receive the vaccine, but what do we do when everyone, but us, has been vaccinated with a vaccine that we are not supposed to even be near a person who has received the vaccine?

It is advised that I never travel in third world countries, because the risk of developing severe gastroenteritis is too great, and there is limited availability of adequate medical care. Gastroenteritis is infection of the stomach or intestines from a variety of causes, such as ingestion of food or water that is contaminated with bacteria or virus. In a healthy individual, this is a minor inconvenience but for a transplant recipient, it can have grave consequences.

When I get dental work done, even my teeth cleaned, I must take a broad spectrum antibiotic beforehand.

Animals carry diseases that could be harmful if transmitted to a recipient, and you should never let them sleep in your bed or lick your face. Notice I changed to *you* as the pronoun instead of *I*. I won't be having a cat or dog in my house, let alone in my bed, and not too near me in your house. That rule was already in effect before I received a transplant, and it had nothing to do with my being allergic to them. They are cute to look at, but they immediately become ugly if they touch me. Cats can be exceptionally harmful, and a transplant recipient should never empty a cat's litter box or allow the cat to climb on a counter top. I have no trouble with these rules, as I would never empty a cat's litter box nor let one climb on my counter top. As nice as I am, a kitty on my counter top might meet with sudden death, if I could do it without touching him. There are pets to avoid at all costs that are more likely to carry disease; stray animals, animals with diarrhea, sick animals, exotic animals and primates (monkeys.) Those who have pets have strict guidelines for safety.

For transplant patients, smoking is discouraged and is far above animals in my house on my list of things to hate. At the backdoor there is a sign that reads, "If your smoking in here, you'd better be on fire." At the front door, there is a sign that reads "No Smoking" but then everyone already knows at Barb's house, smoking is not allowed.

Because of antirejection medications, I am advised to stay out of the sun because of my chance of getting some types of cancer, especially skin cancer, but my risk is heightened so I now comply even more than I did before my transplant when I used sunscreen and avoided sun exposure due to my fair skin and a general belief that everyone should avoid it as much as possible to prevent skin cancer. I use sunscreen if I must, but I prefer to avoid the sun where possible. I have firmly set in my brain that everything we breathe, put on our skin or in our bodies goes through our livers.

I am told to stay out of public swimming pools until a year post transplant. I do not have a problem with this but many patients do.

These restrictions do not change later; they are forever, much like "til death do us part" but without the chance of divorce.

Men who may have been impotent when their liver function was poor may find that sexual function usually returns. Females whose menstrual cycles have been absent during their liver disease will usually see it return within a few months after transplant. Sorry, ladies, but in the sex department, post transplant men get a better deal; unless you're lucky enough to have the side effect of antirejection medications that I have missed so far and a partner to play with. I define luck as when preparedness meets opportunity so as I have said before I am prepared for this too.

Even with all the limitations, suggestions and rules of the new regime, I cannot quit living my life, or the transplant would make me as I was before when I could not leave the house. I do not take the rules, suggestions and limitations lightly. I take the necessary precautions, plus a few more, and work within them. I do not fight them. I go with the flow. There are going to be illnesses that come my way in spite of all I do to prevent them. When they do, I will deal with them.

The transplant ordeal is so enormous that I cannot imagine that anyone who goes through the process would take a chance to reject or infect by not protecting the body the transplant is housed in within a cradle of responsibility. I avoid even the people closest to me, if they have a cold or any contagious infection. An illness benign to a healthy person is violent, antagonistic and deadly for an immunosuppressed person.

Immunosuppressive, antirejection drugs have unpleasant side effects. Everyday, to keep my body from rejecting Terry's liver that is still foreign to it, I put into my body cyclosporin and Prednisolone that lower it's ability to fight off infections but to insist that my body like Terry's liver. I find it ironic that what can make me physically worse also saves my life and that the good-guy steroids that make my body like Terry's liver as much as I do are also the bad guys with so many side effects that betray my immune system, and the T cells that were damaged by the disease before are now purposely suppressed. Without the antirejection medications, the T cells would return to their war on foreign objects in my body, one of which is Terry's liver.

Antirejection drugs only provide protection for a specific amount of time in your body before they "wear off." During this time, your body gradually "breaks down" the dose and removes it from your system. Another dose is needed to continue protection. For my medication, that amount of time is twelve hours. Cyclosporin must be taken not twice daily, but every twelve hours. I am careful to take my medications precisely on time. The results for not adhering to my strict drug therapy are rejection of my prized possession or death; so when I am inclined to sleep late in the morning, I ask myself *do I want to live or die.* I have gone through too much to chance it. On days when I feel rather lazy and my silent reply to that mental question is "I'm so comfortable," I ask it again and always get up and take my medication. Before I received my transplant, I was not finished with living. I am still not finished.

At a year post transplant, when I suffered a rejection, my sister Betty asked me if I had it to do all over again, would I do it. I responded, "Yes, and if I have to do it again, I am going for it." She replied, "Oh-my-God, I think I'll commit suicide if you have to have another one." When I told my niece, Destiny, what her Aunt Betty had said, she asked, "Did you tell her to leave her liver for you?" Sometimes, you have to laugh to breathe.

During the time of my illness, surgery and recovery, all my friends met and bonded. When I speak of one of them to another, I no longer need to refer to April as "the friend whose family I lived with before James and I married " or to Sherri as "my cousin's wife" or to Joann as "the one with the black hair" or to Ben as "Donna's mother." They ask about each other often, and some of them keep in touch with each other.

In Terry's and my recycled life, I am focused on the road ahead. Without him and the transplant, I had slipped through the crack of life and would have missed that road.

There are those who made parts of this journey with me who feel like they know the outcome. May I remind you we never know the outcome?

Many times throughout life I have had the thought "this is the worst thing that can ever happen to me. I won't ever have to go through anything this bad again." I was wrong. I did not think it when I lost my mother when I was but twelve, but when I was thirty, I thought that her death and my not being able to conceive a child of my own were the worst experiences I would ever have in life. I thought that I was set to live the rest of my life with the worst tragedies behind me. I thought I had surely paid my dues. Later I was diagnosed with lupus and I had that thought again. Then, my neck was broken in a car accident. I was convinced that was the worst thing I would encounter. Then my marriage broke up. Then I learned that I had a deadly liver disease to face alone. The worst things that could happen to me may or may not have happened already, but one thing I know for sure is that the best thing has happened. I feel I was a handed a death sentence that has been overturned.

There are those who say that transplant trades one set of problems for another. The difference is you live with the new ones, with the old ones you die. It is a matter of sometimes you make the right decision and sometimes you make the decision right. Making the decision right is changing your lifestyle to fit the new regime of medications and all that goes with it. Even with all the changes in my life, I am the same, only healthier.

I suspected all along, while growing up after the death of my mother, that I could take anything—and after the last decade of my life where I had a lumpectomy, a broken neck, surgery to remove spurs from both feet, gallbladder surgery, the breakup of my thirty year marriage, diagnosis of end-stage liver disease, a liver transplant with a second surgery afterwards, a stroke, two rejection episodes, and all that goes with it—I have decided, with God's help, I can. By now, He must surely be thinking, "There she is *again*."

You take the good things in life and run with them. In my case, the good thing is sharing life with an angel I never met, Terry Sharp. Eventually God will say "come home" to every transplant recipient, and that does include me. Until then, I am living my extended life, given freely to me by Terry and his family.

If you could save someone's life, would you do it? What if you could save or enhance as many as fifty lives? You can as an organ and tissue donor.

In the year 2010, one in every ten American's will need or have had an organ transplant. One of those can be you or one of your loved ones; just in case, you or one of your loved ones needs a transplant or in case your life ends with brain death and you can be someone's miracle, talk to your family. Your family will be notified and asked about your decision, so the most important thing you can do—more important than placing a sticker on your driving license or carrying a signed donor card, is to make sure your family is aware you want to be a donor. Your family must consent for you to be a donor.

I have fallen, but with the help of many, I have gotten up. Life is not going to pass me by after all. I consider these years of illness as a stutter in my life. Stutters in life are necessary to make us see better the things we appreciate. Now I have a need to make the most of life and apparently that no longer includes housework, which I was such a stickler about before.

There is another timeline in my life to go with others that define my life. My life is now separated into categories of before Mama died, after I married, before the car accident, when I was married, when I was sick, and now after the transplant, along with others that didn't have the impact those times had.

I am a self-appointed missionary and proselytizer for donor awareness. I write articles for magazines and newspapers and give speeches telling others about my transplant experience in my choppy, country Texas accent. In fact, you would think I was practicing medicine when you come in and see the model of a human liver and a torso with removable organs that I take to presentations so children can see what the organs look like and where they are located. A doctor I have never met, Dr. Mark Grebenau, learned that I wanted to buy the organ models and donated these two models to me. Angels are everywhere.

If you want to start helping others, yourself, or your loved one who may one day need transplantation surgery, invite me or other recipients to speak about organ donation to any groups—church groups, women's groups, school groups, social groups—you are in or call your local organ procurement agency and ask them to send a speaker. They have volunteer speakers, who are no longer dying to, but who are eager to tell their story and inform you about organ and tissue donation.

My miracle began long before I received that call on the rainy morning of October 6, 2000. It began when something happened in Terry's life that caused him to tell his wife, Nancy, what his wishes were. He had been made aware of organ donation through literature, TV or a transplant event someone told him about. That awareness put my miracle in motion, possibly even before I needed a transplant. However, without my donor conveying his wishes to his wife, my miracle might not ever have happened at all.

It takes one miracle when you are in need of an organ, but when you donate you are part of several miracles.

I was the blessed recipient of Terry Sharp's liver; others recipients also received miracles from this generous man and his family.

With all my pain and loss, as my world stood still in chronic disease, I still feel blessed. As I relayed to my donor family in the poem I wrote for them, these events were not happenstance. God planned my life, and he planned Terry's life too. My donor and his family allowed my miracle to happen, and I am a representation of his being. I try to live my life accordingly. I have found my niche and passion in life in my writing and speaking.

Transplant is a credit to fate, luck, destiny, surgical skill and lots of prayer all of which I am a recipient of, along with Terry's liver and all of which I am eternally grateful.

I now live life as everyone else lives it, in the present, one day at a time. It is great to live it that way instead of five minutes at a time as I had to for so long.

The day will come when God will say come home to me as well. But, in the meantime, I am blessed with the gift of celebrating life as a member of a time-share with Terry, who is so real, keeping me alive. And that in itself is a miracle every day.

Although I no longer feel that Terry is imaginary; he is real to me in every way. Sometimes I think of him as Adam—when God caused him to fall into a deep sleep; and while he was sleeping he took one of his ribs. Then the Lord God made a woman out of the rib he had taken out of the man. Only, in Terry's case He recycled a woman with his liver.

Still after almost two years, I hurry, impatient to join the show of life. If you see me walking across a parking lot, even from out by the tree, at the Paris Wal-Mart, what I am thinking is "I can't believe I can do this!" I think that thought every time even when someone is walking with me and one of us is talking.

I feel like I have gone home again. Home, the place where you can go where all your eccentricities are not noticed. I feel like I've reached a place of redemption, where life was lost and then regained.

Now, often when someone asks me, "How are you" my reply is not "I'm just great" it is "I am just great!" And, if it is someone very close to me, they can tell.

My expectations for feeling great have changed also. Feeling great no longer means I am on top of the world, feeling wonderfully young and able physically to do anything I want. It means I feel well enough to accomplish the necessary tasks to run my slower, but fuller, life that I share with Terry because of his family's generosity. My priorities have changed. What used to seem extremely important is now relegated to a lower rung on my ladder of things to do.

When I think back to the time so very long ago when I was a young healthy woman, I am saddened at the time lost to illness; however, back then I didn't even appreciate my own potty.

Not The End
And, that is why transplants are miracles!

Information Resources

You cannot be too informed; time to learn is time well spent.

United Network for Organ Sharing (UNOS)
1100 Boulders Parkway, #500
Richmond, VA 23225
Phone: 804-330-8500
Toll free Patient Transplant Information: 1-888-894-6361
Toll free Donor Information: 1-888-355-SHARE
Website: www.unos.org
Patient Email: www.patients.unos.org

Amber Pharmacy
amber@amberpharmacy.com

American Liver Foundation
75 Maiden Lane
New York, NY 10028
Phone: 212-668-1000
Toll free: 1-800-GO-LIVER (465-4837)
Fax: 212-483-8179
Website: www.liverfoundation.org
Email: webmail@liverfoundation.org

American Association for the Study of Liver Disease (AASLD)
1729 King Street, #100
Alexandria, VA 22314
Phone: 703-299-9766
Fax: 703-299-9622
Website: www.aasld.org
Email: www.aasld@aasld.org

American Gastroenterological Association (AGA)
7910 Woodmont, #700
Bethesda, MD 20814
Phone: 301-654-2055
Website: www.gastro.org
Email: www.webinfo@gasro.org

Baylor Health Care Systems
Transplant Services, 4th Floor Roberts
3500 Gaston Ave
Dallas, TX 754246
Phone: 214-820-2050
Fax: 214-820-4527
www.bhcs.com

Centers for Disease Control and Prevention (CDC)
Hepatitis Branch
1600 Clifton Road, NE
Atlanta, GA 30333
Phone: 404-639-3534
Toll free Hepatitis Information Line: 1-888-443-7232
Website: www.cdc.gov
Email: Available at the cdc.gov website

Children's Organ Transplant Association (COTA)
2501 COTA Drive
Bloomington, IN 47403
Toll free: 1-800-366-2682
Website: www.cota.org
Email: Jennifer@cota.org

CVS ProCare Pharmacy
Toll free: 1-800-238-7828
Website: www.cvsprocare.com

Hepatitis Education Project
4603 Aurora Avenue North
Seattle, WA 98103
Toll free: 1-800-218-6932
Phone: 206-732-0311
Fax: 206-732-0312
Website: www.scn.org/health/hepatitis
Email: www.hep@scn.org

Hepatitis C Education and Support Network
P.O. Box 1231
Locust Grove, VA 22508
Phone: 540-972-2856
Fax: 540-972-4493
Website: www.hepcesn.org
Email: www.hepcesn@hepcesn.org

Hepatitis C Global Foundation
1404 Madison Ave
Redwood City, CA 94061-1550
Phone: 650-369-0330
Fax: 650-369-0331
Website: www.hepcglobal.org
Email: jtranchina@hepcglobal.org

Hepatitis C Support Project
P.O. Box 427037
San Francisco, CA 94142
Phone: 415-978-2400
Website: www.hcadvocate.org
Email: www.sfhepcat@pacbell.net

The Hep C Connection
1177 Grant Street, #200
Denver, CO 80203
Toll free: Hep C Hotline 1-800-522-4372
Website: www.hepc-connection.org
Email: info@hepc-connection.org

Hepatitis Foundation International (HFI)
504 Blick Drive
Silver Spring, MD 20904
Toll free: 1-800-891-0707
Website: www.hepfi.org
Email: TKT@hepfi.org

Latino Organization for Liver Awareness (LOLA)
P.O. Box 842
Throngs Neck Station
Bronx, New York 10465
Toll free: 1-888-367-5652
Website: www.lola-national.org
Email: mdlola@aol.com

Medical Information Resources
377 West 5250 South
Ogden, UT 84405
Toll free: 1-888-203-6062
Website: www.medicalfundraising.org

Merck Manual of Medical Information
(For the layperson)
www.merckhomeedition.com

Minority Organ Tissue Transplant Education Program (MOTTEP)
2041 Georgia Avenue NW, Suite 3100
Washington, DC 20060
Phone: 202-865-4888
Toll free: 800-393-2839
Fax: 202-865-4880
Website: www.nationalmottep.org

National Foundation for Transplants
1102 Brookfield, #200
Memphis, TN 38119
Toll free: 1-800-489-3863
Website: www.transplants.org

National Transplant Assistance Fund
3475 West Chester Pike, #230
Newtown Square, PA 19073
Toll free: 1-800-642-8399
Phone: 610-353-9684
Fax: 610-353-1616
Website: www.transplantfund.org
Email: NTAF@transplantfund.org

National Institutes of Health (NIH)
2 Information Way
Bethesda, MD 20892-3570
Phone: 301-654-3810
Toll free: 1-800-891-5389
Website: www.niddk.nih.gov/health/digest.htm
Email: nddic@info.niddk.nih.gov

National Transplant Society (NTS)
3340 Dundee Road, Unit 2C-3
Northbrook, IL 60062-2331
Phone: 847-412-0604
Fax: 847-291- 9284
Website: www.organdonor.org
Email: NTS@organdonor.org

Novartis Pharmaceuticals
Mark D. Grebenau, MD, PhD
Transplant Business Unit
Novartis Pharmaceuticals
One Health Plaza
East Hanover, NJ 07936
Toll free: 1-800-669-6682 (NOW-NOVA)
Website: www.transplantsquare.com
Novartis' Transplant Learning Center (TLC)
1-888-852-3683

Parents of Kids with Infectious Diseases (PKIDS)
P.O. Box 5666
Vancouver, WA 98668
Phone: 360-695-0293
Fax: 360-695-6941
Website: www.pkids.org
Email: www.pkids@pkids.org

Roche Laboratories
Transplant Partnering Program (TPPP)
www.tppp.net

Southwest Transplant Alliance
3110 Rawlins, #1100
Dallas, TX 75219
Phone: 214-522-0255
Toll free: 1-800-788-8058
Website: www.organ.org

TransWeb Organ Transplantation Information Site (TRIO)
2117 L. St. NW, #353
Washington, DC 20037-1524
Phone: 202-293-0980
Toll free: 1-800-974-6386
Email: www.pskardatrio@aol.com

Texas Liver Coalition
One Riverway, #2460
Houston, TX 77056
Phone: 713-626-4959
Toll free: 1-800-725-4837
Fax: 713-626-4960
Website: www.texasliver.org
Email: www.mail@texasliver.org

Veterans Aimed Toward Awareness
Veteranshepaware.com

169

Your Family Must Sign For You to Donate

Here, on the last page of this book, where it will be all right to tear a sheet out, is a letter for your use in bringing up the issue of organ and tissue donation to family members. Tear this page out or make copies of it, as many copies as you need, fill in the blanks then send or give a copy of the signed letter to as many of your family members as you wish; the more family members who know your wishes the more apt those wishes are to be carried out.

A Personal Letter to My Family

Dear _____,

If the occasion occurs, I would like to donate life by being an organ and tissue donor.

I am letting you know my decision to donate life to others because my family members will have to sign for my wishes to be carried out.

Just so you know, I wish to donate the following:

- ❏ **ANY** needed organs and tissue
- ❏ **ONLY** the following organs and tissue:

_____

Thank you for honoring my commitment to donate life through organ and tissue donation and thank you for this personal care. I love you.

Sincerely,

Donor Signature _____

Date _____

Printed in the United States
973300005B